Nature Zentangles

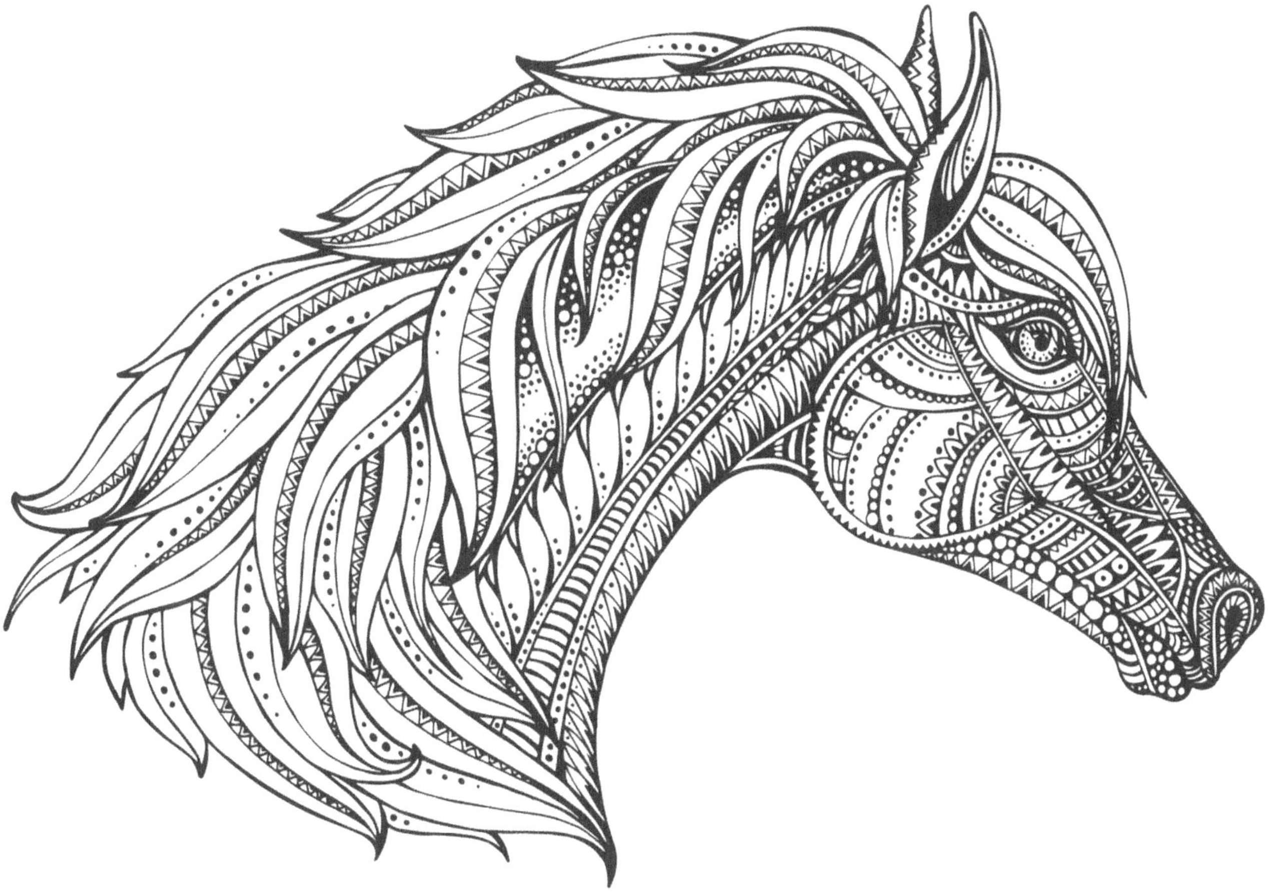

ANIMALS, FLORALS, LANDSCAPES & SEASCAPES

Various Artists
Curated by Samantha West

This addition to Samantha West's series for the experienced colorist is comprised of beautiful designs in a collection of expertly rendered coloring pages. Fifty-two detailed illustrations featuring animals, florals, landscapes and seascapes. Bring them to life with your personal coloring style for hours of relaxation and entertainment. The single-sided pages allow you to experiment with different media and makes displaying your finished creations a breeze.

International Standard Book Number
ISBN-13: 978-1539903970
ISBN-10: 1539903974

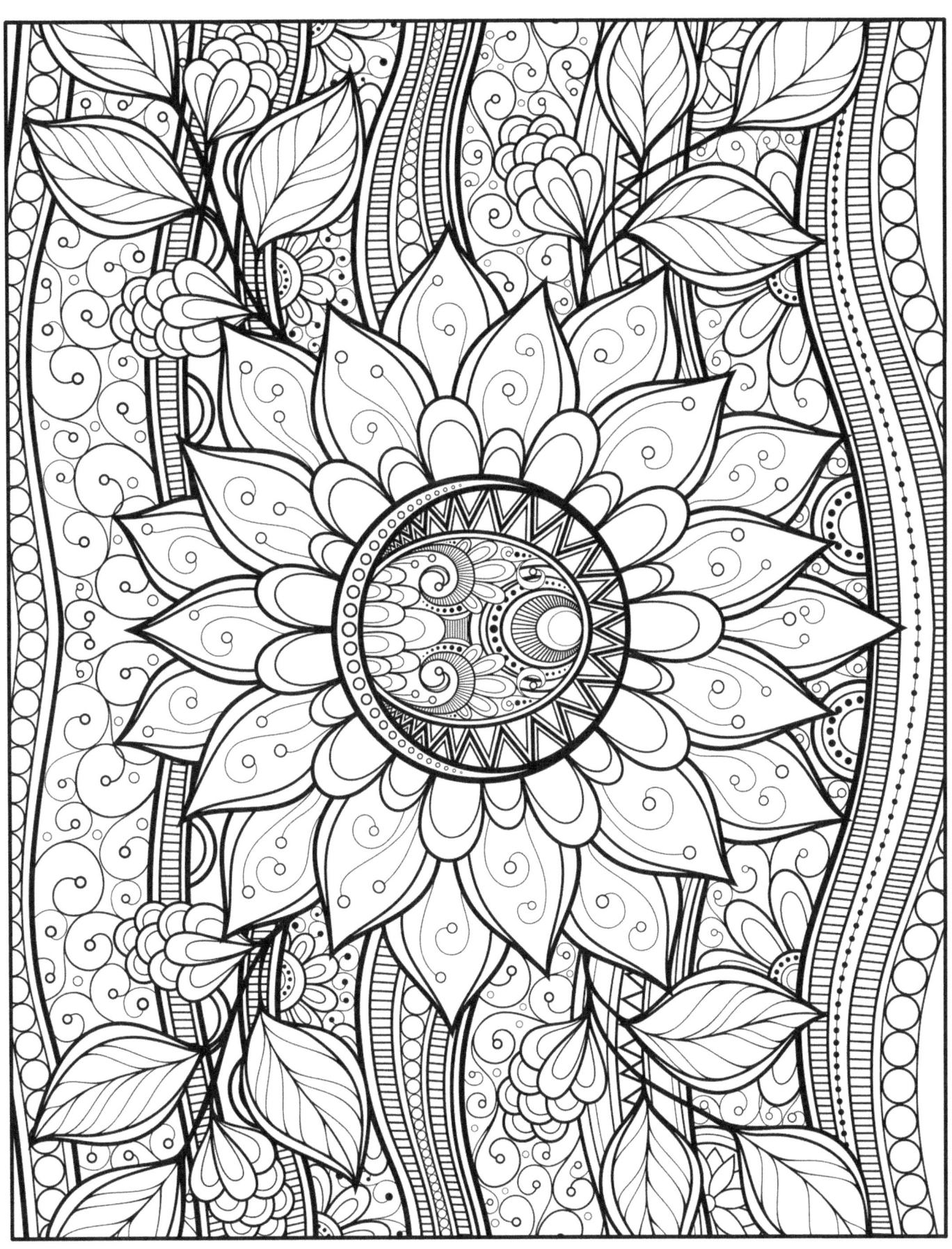

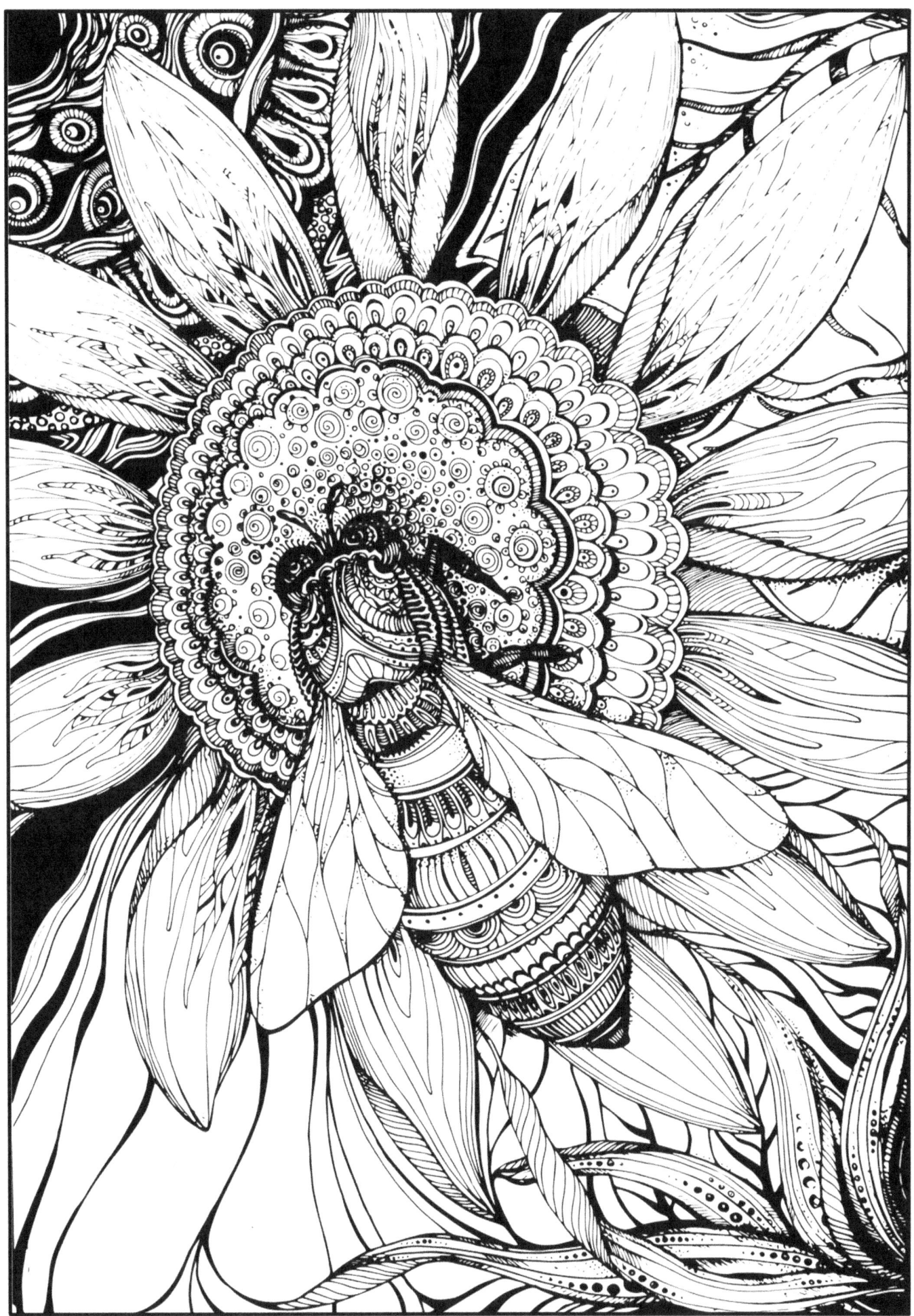

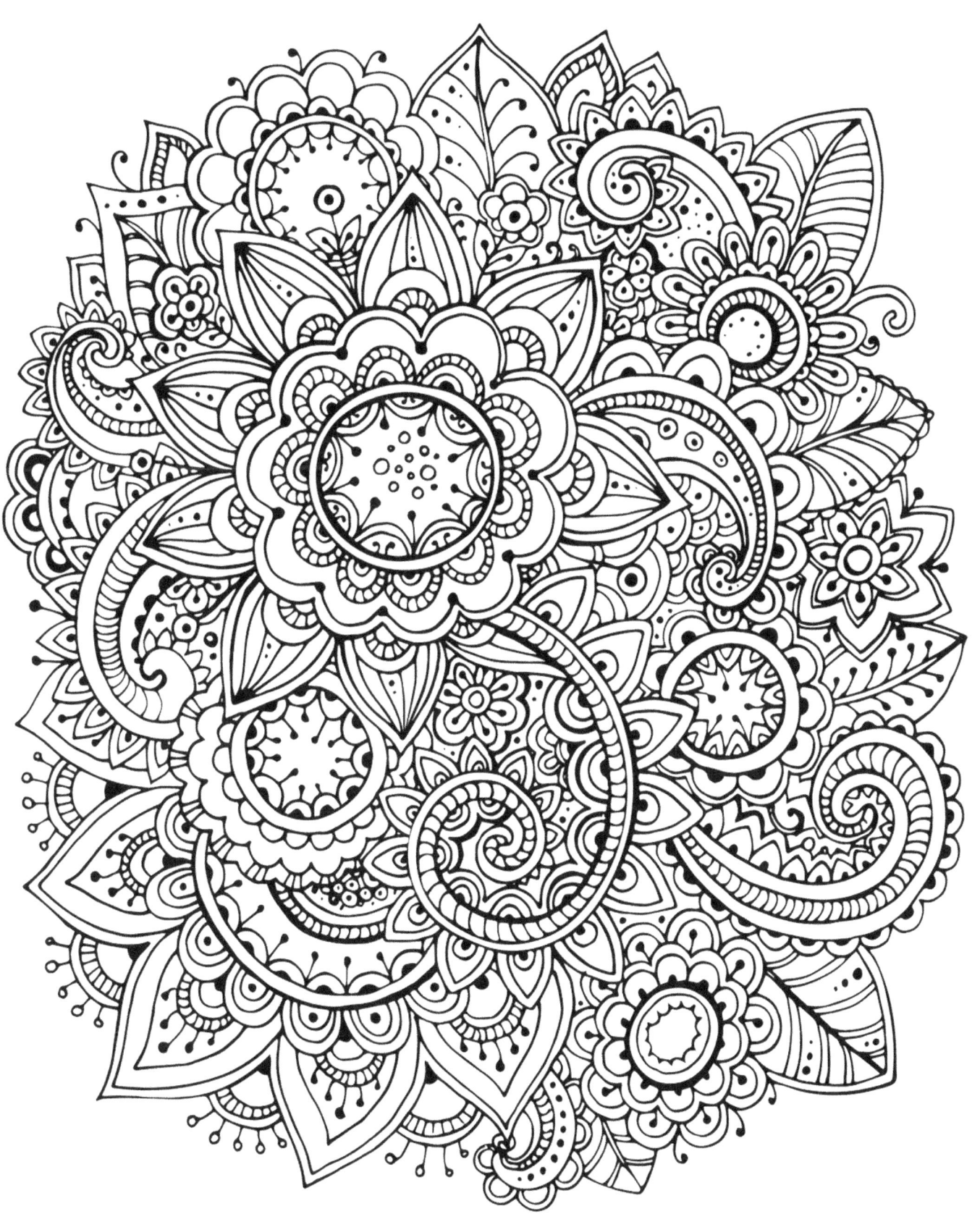

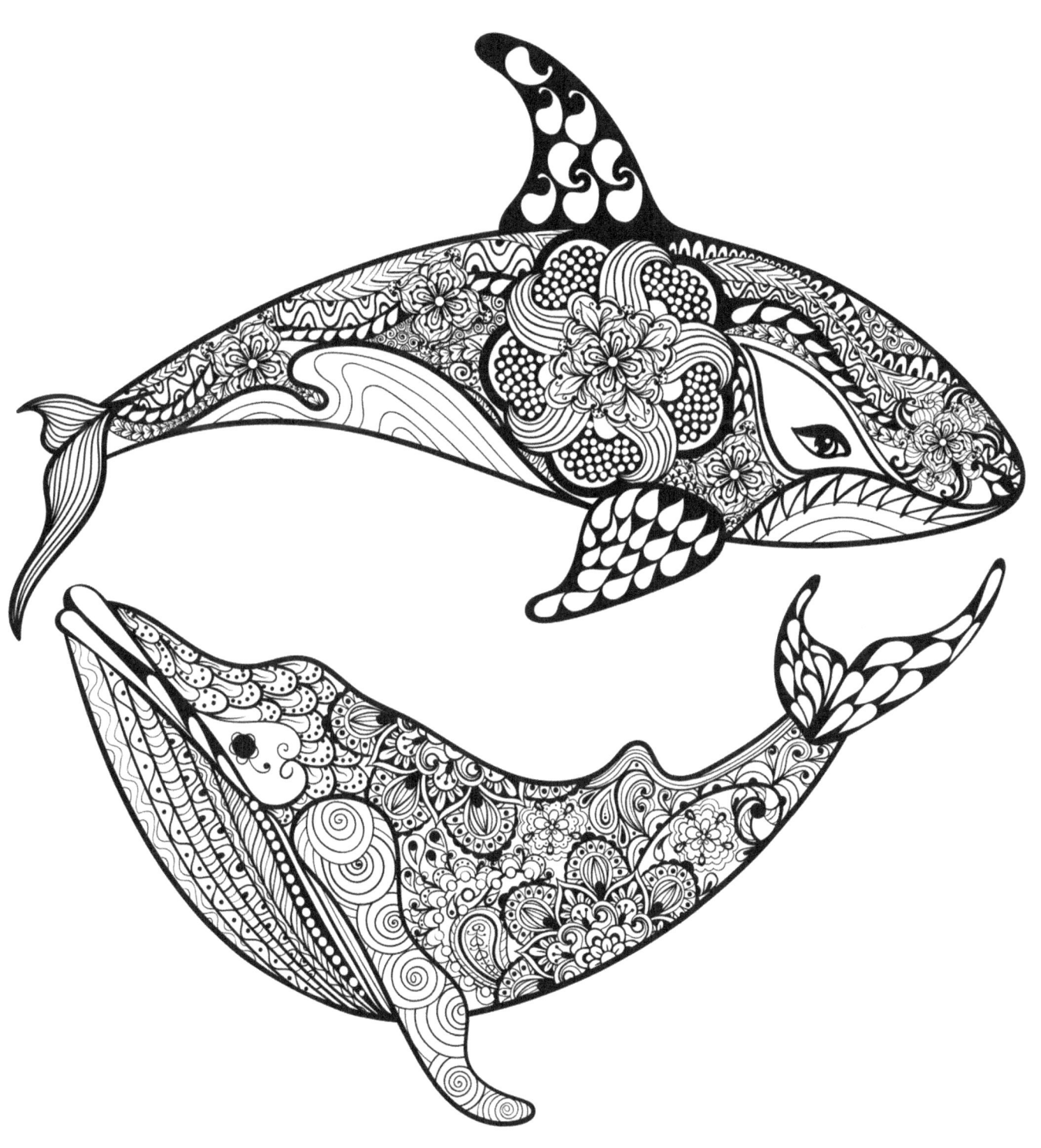

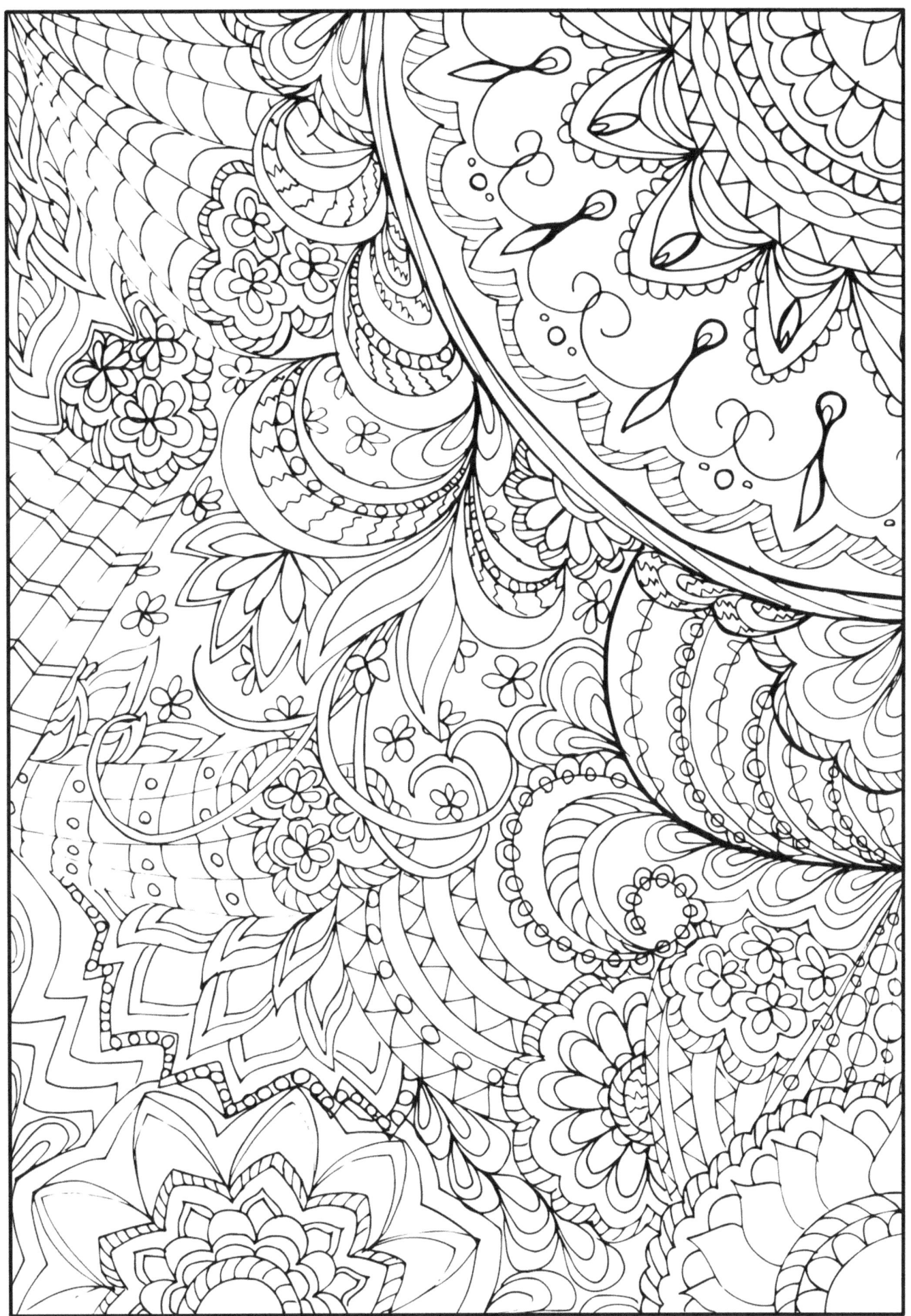

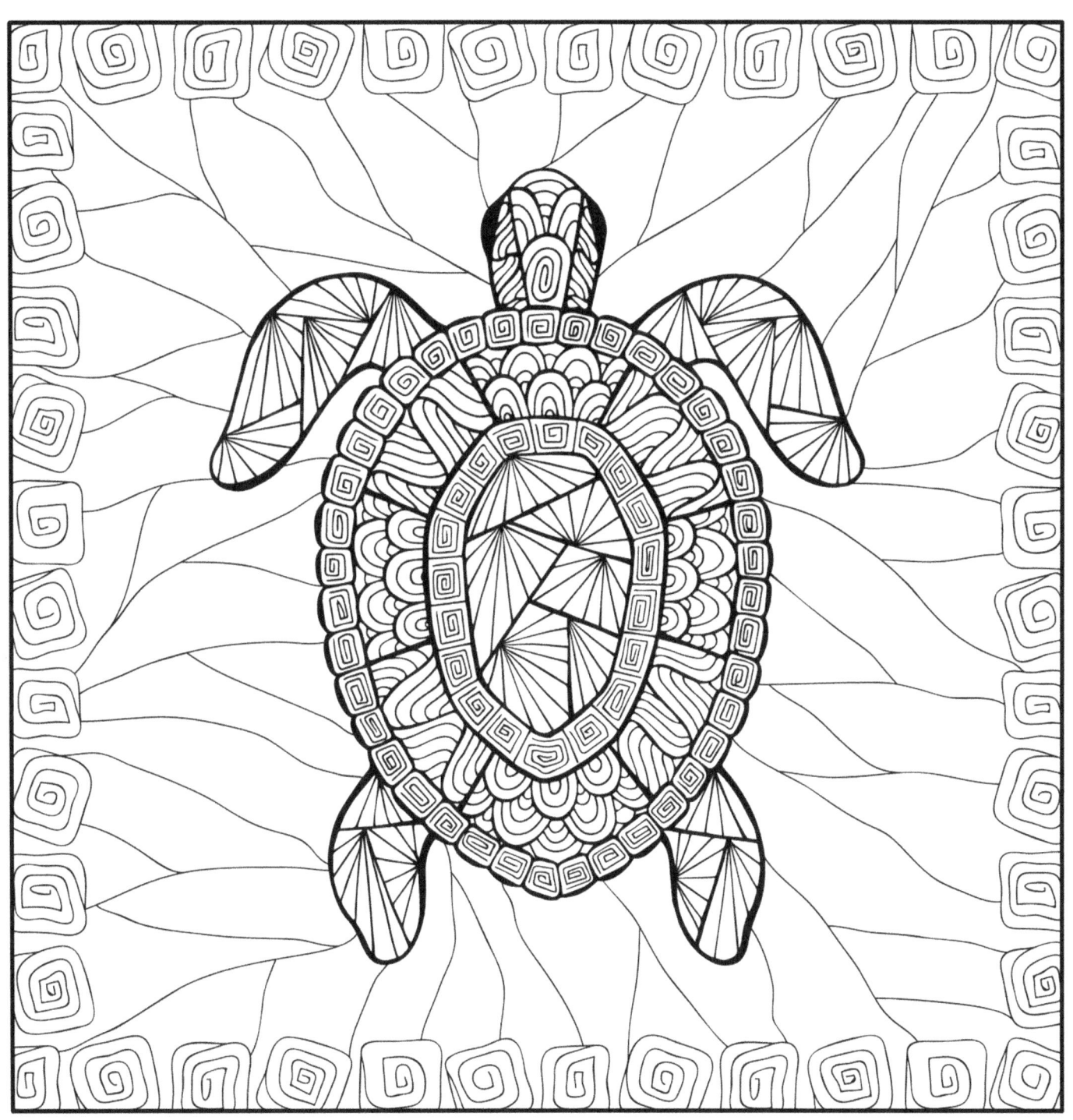

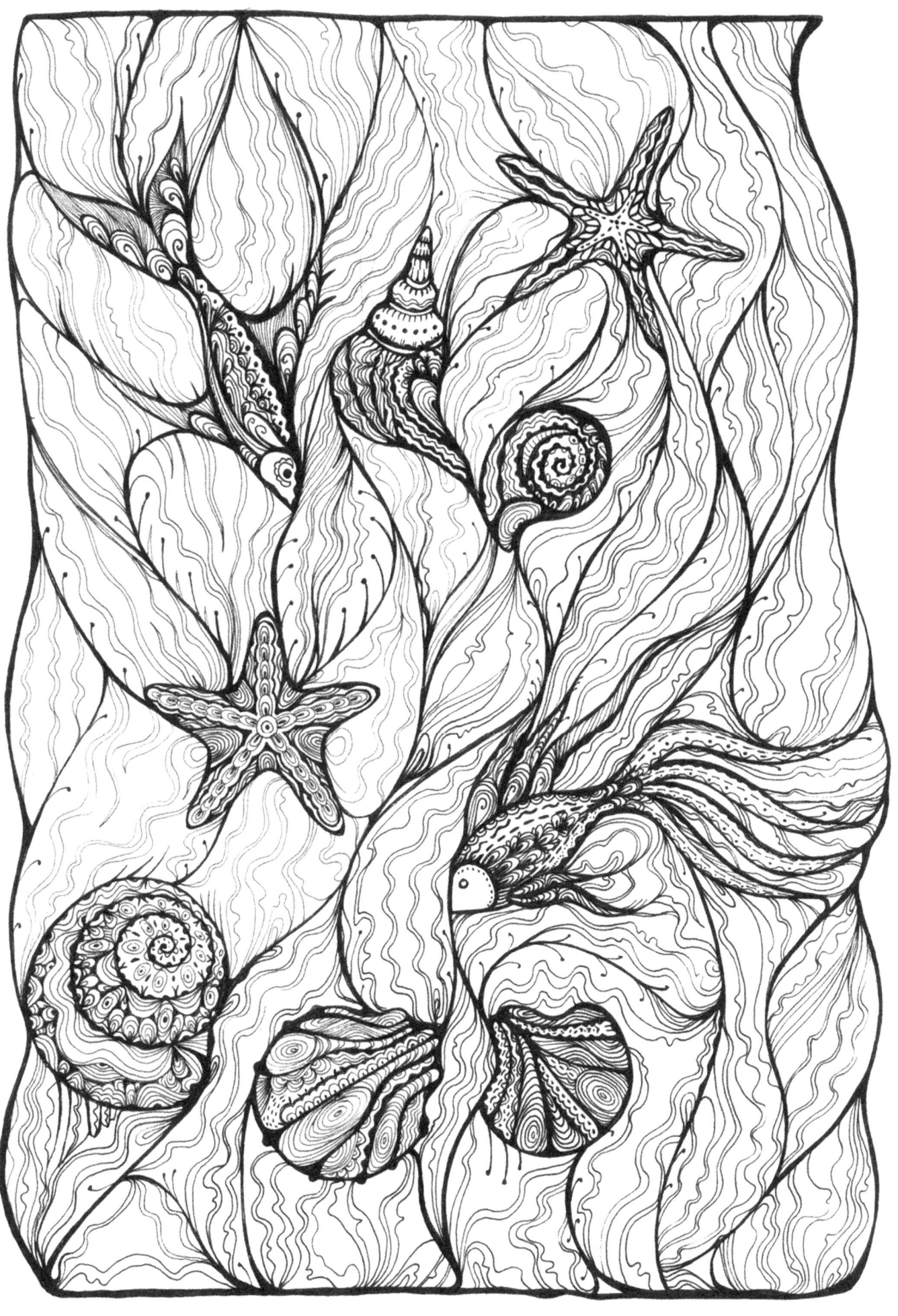

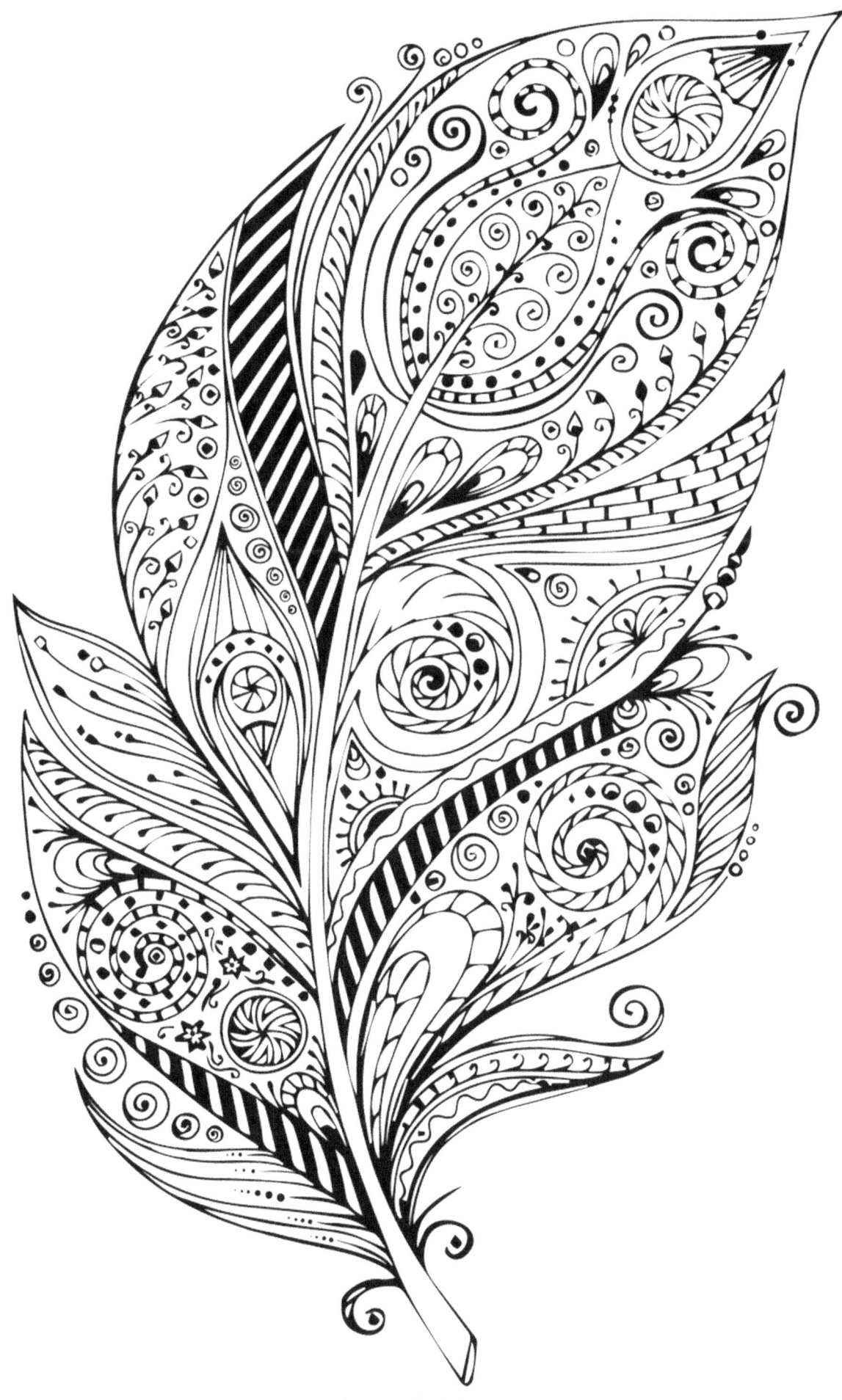

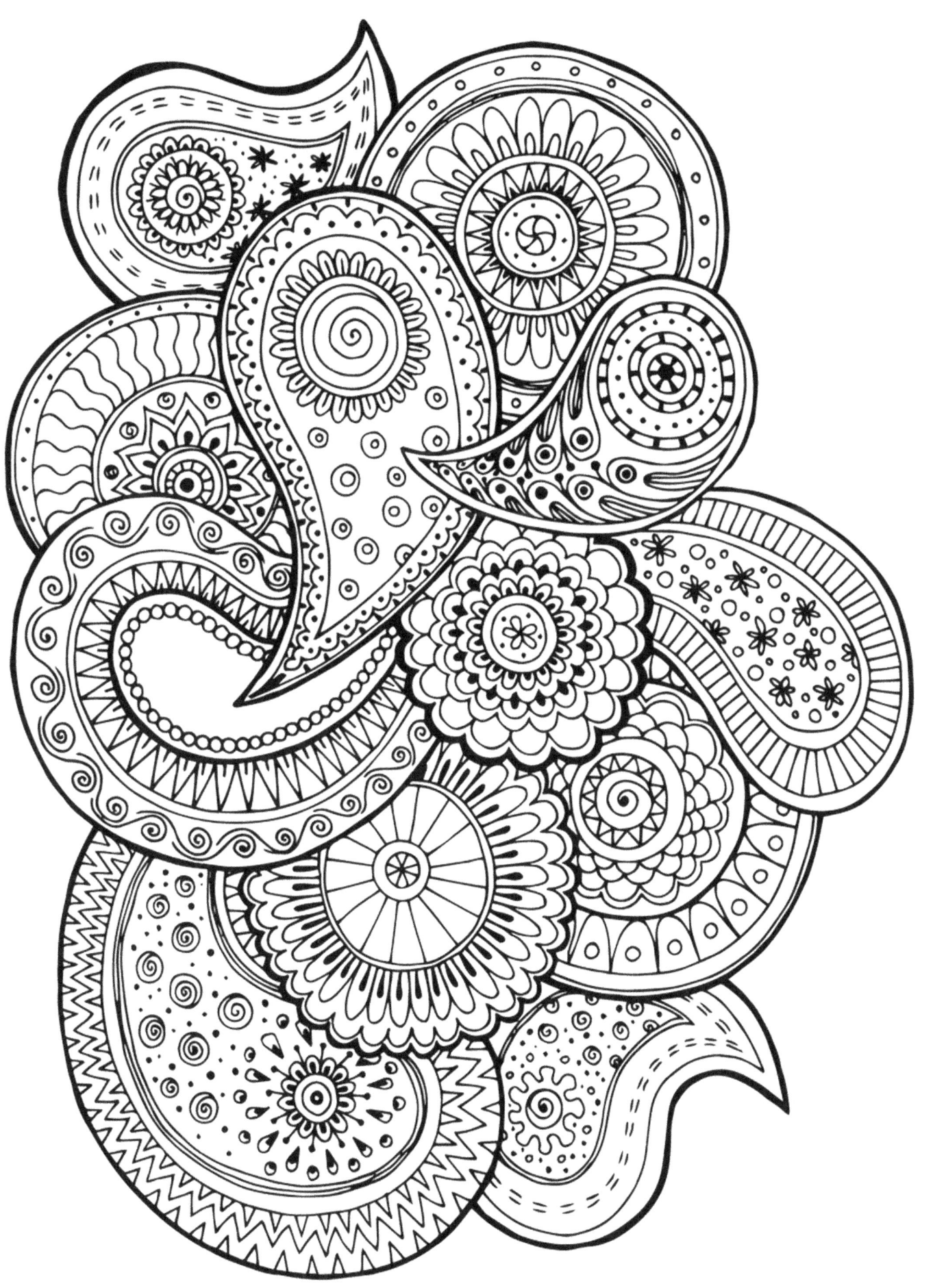

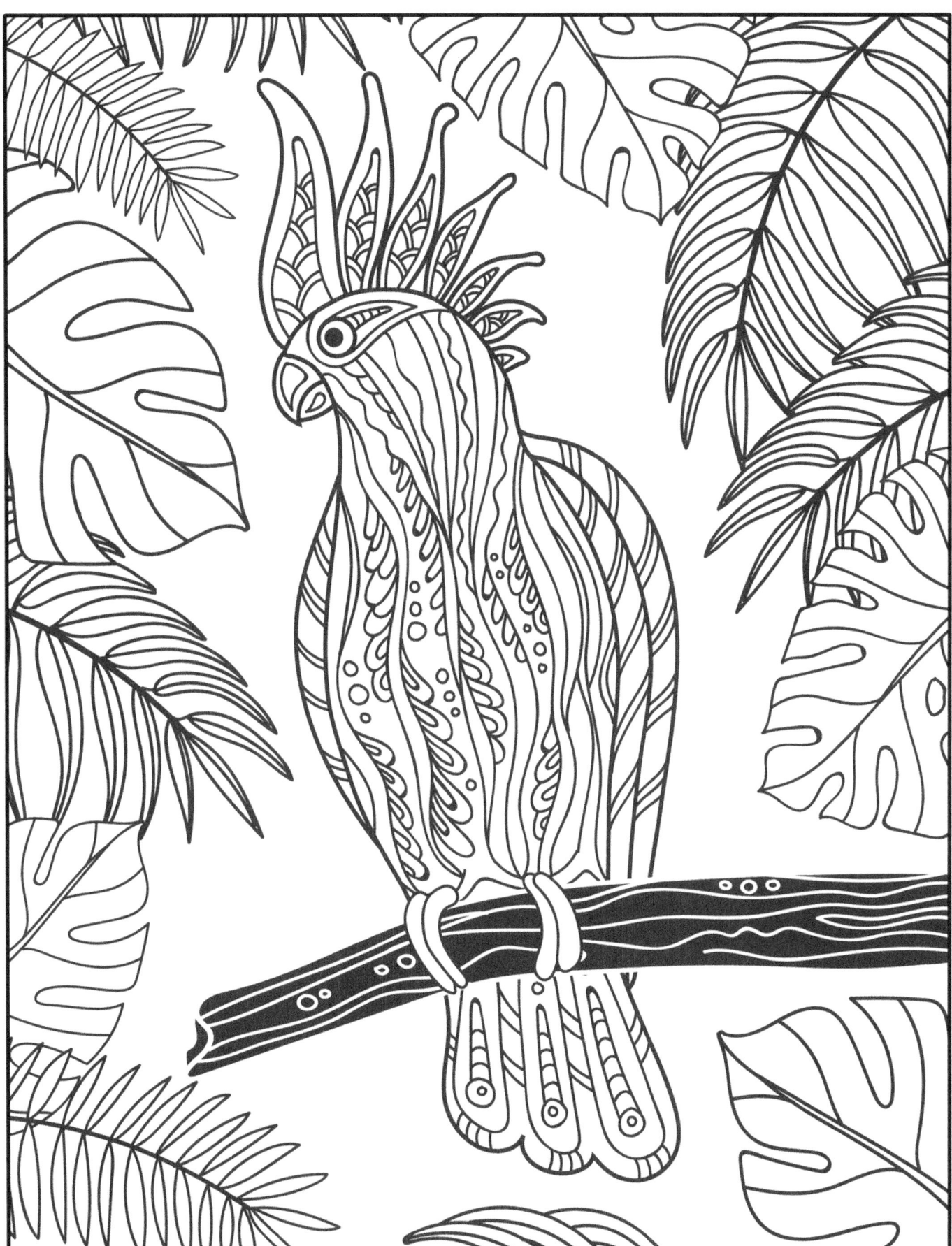

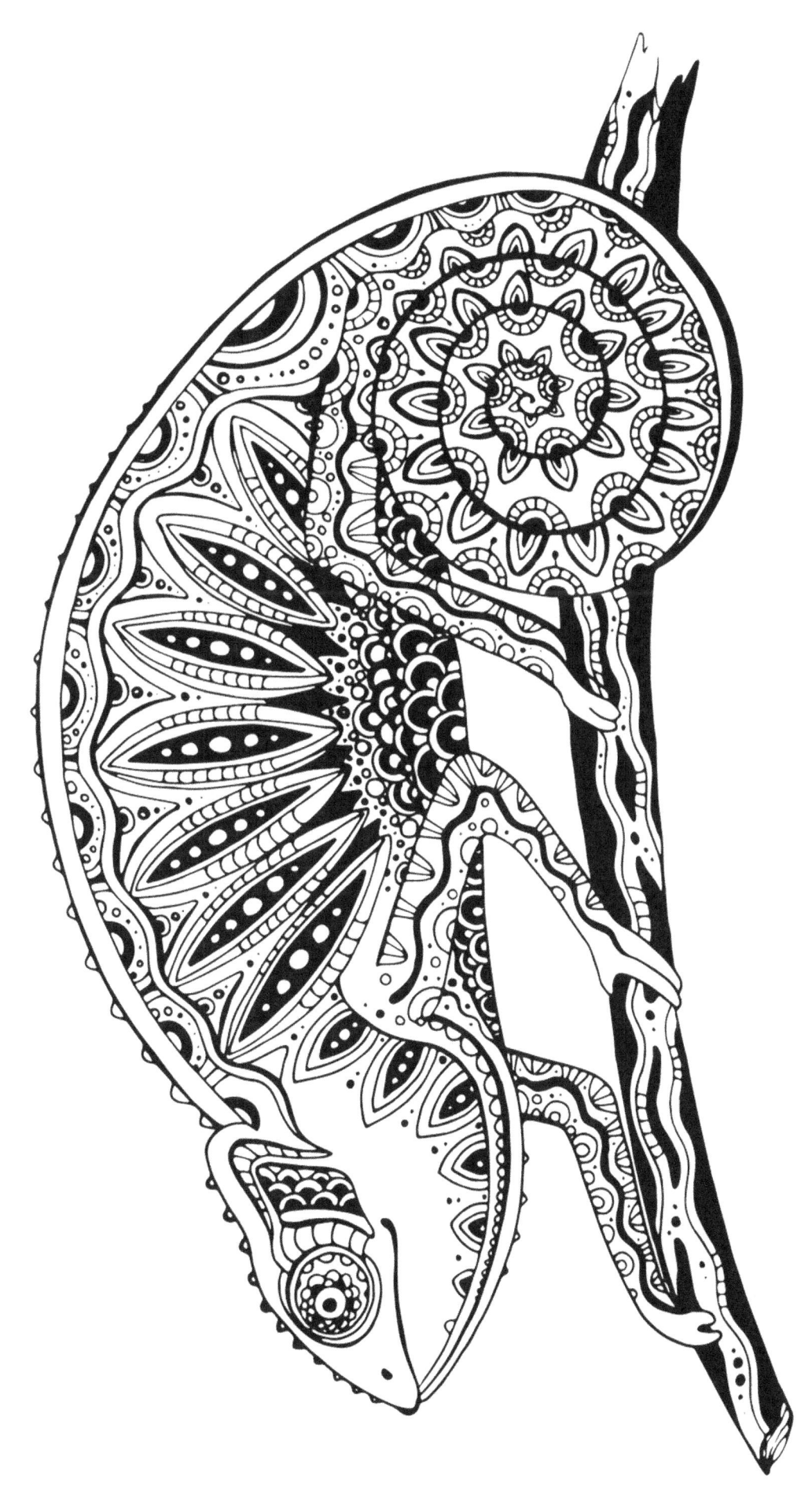

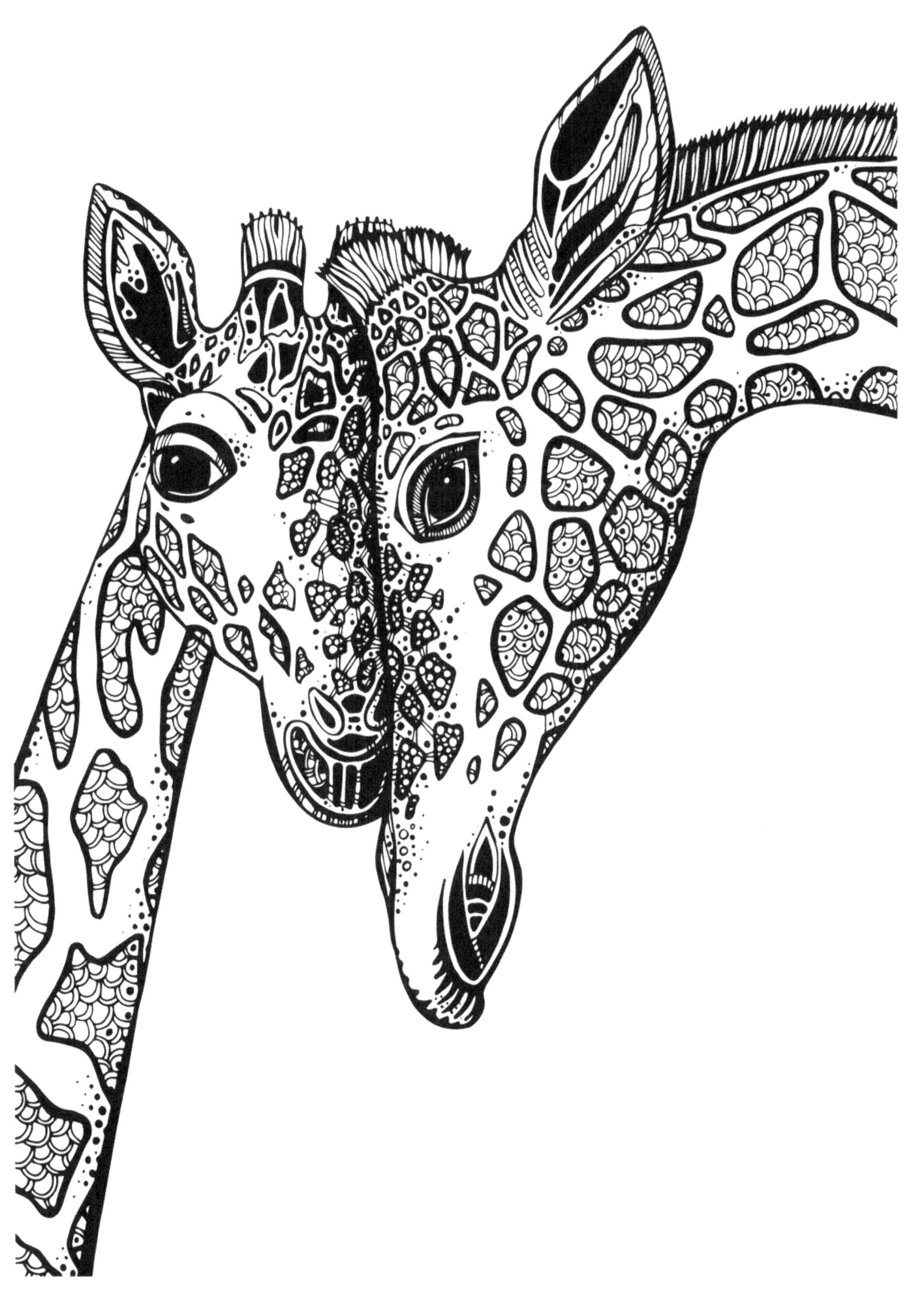

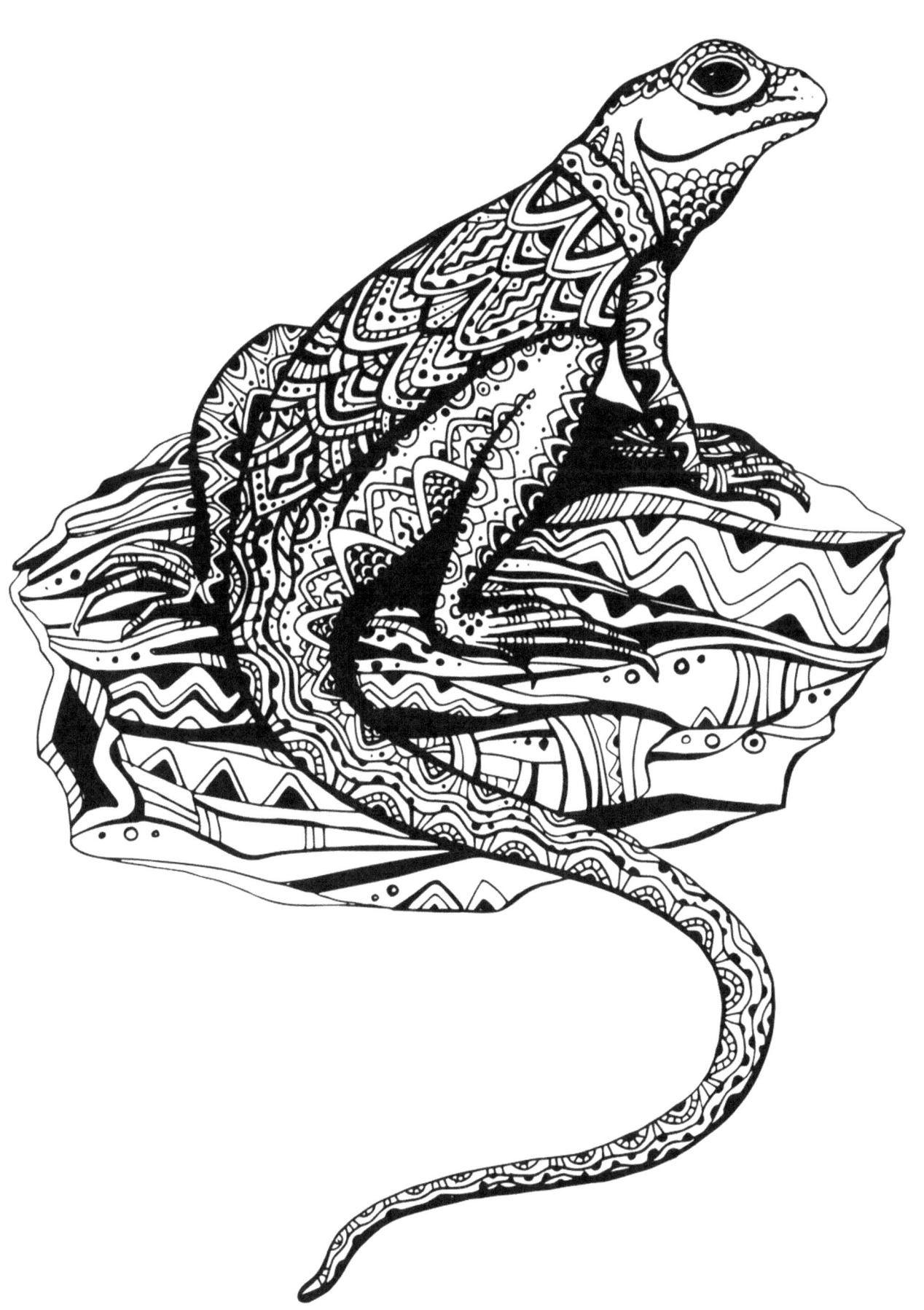

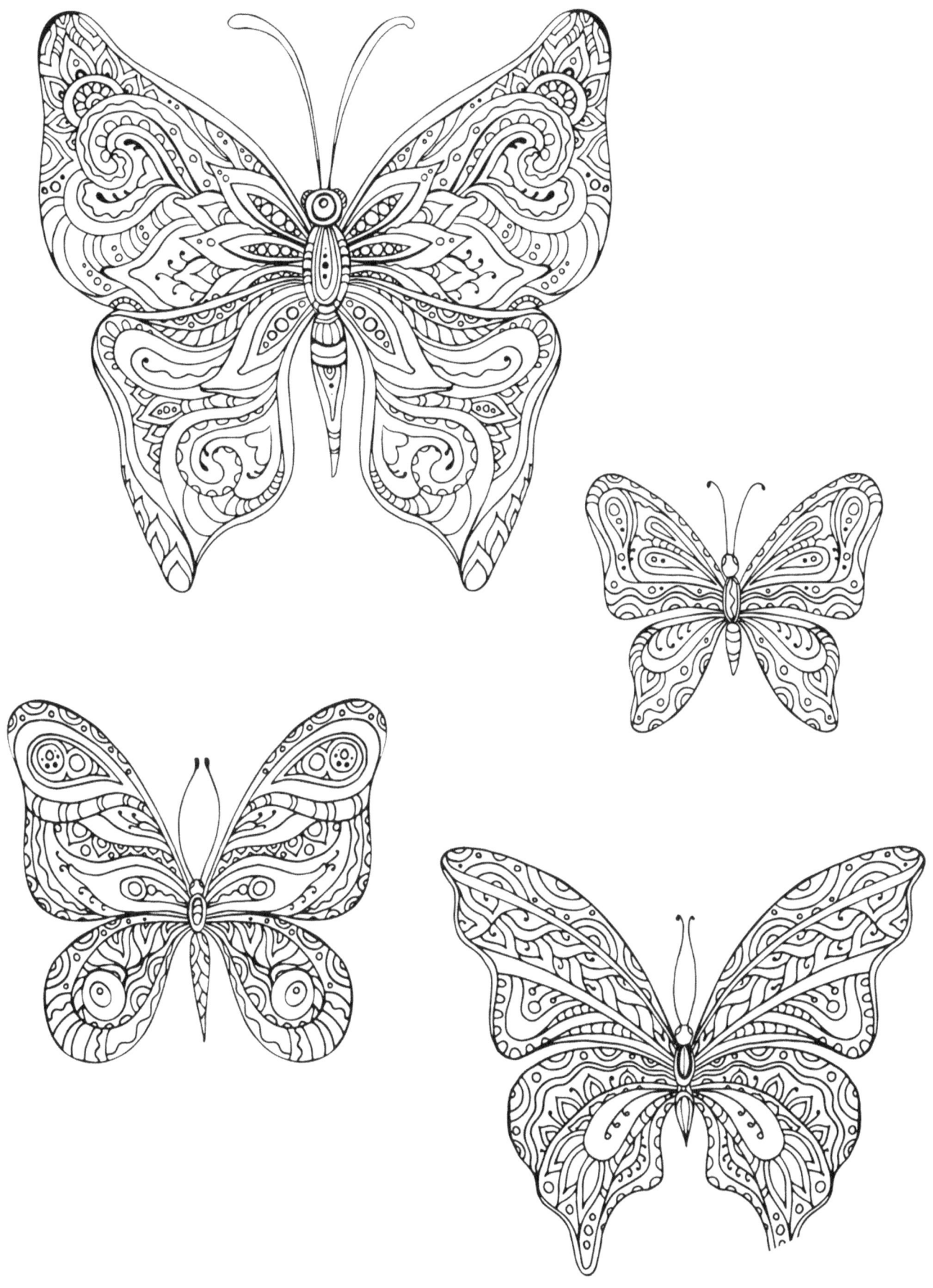

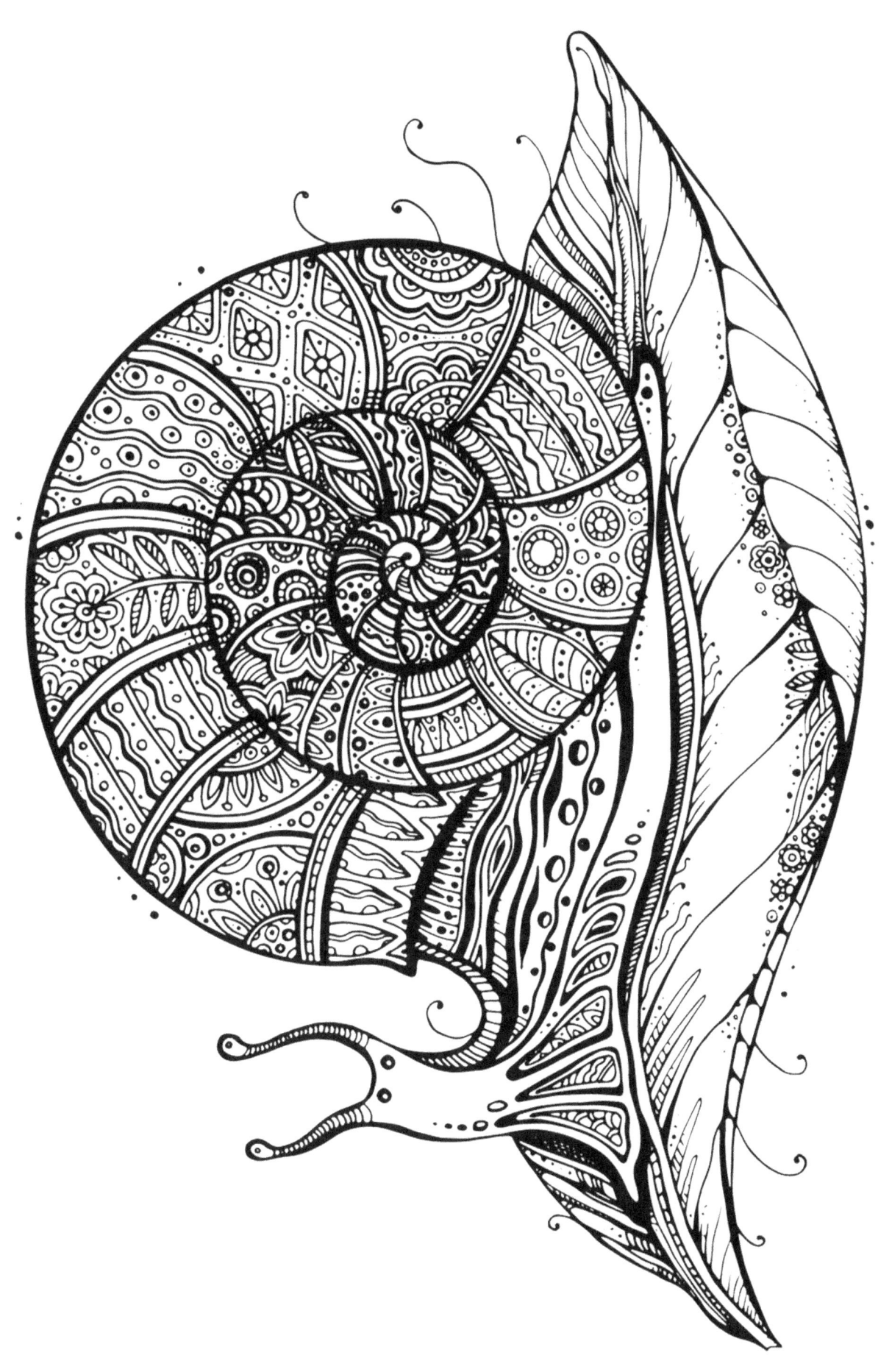

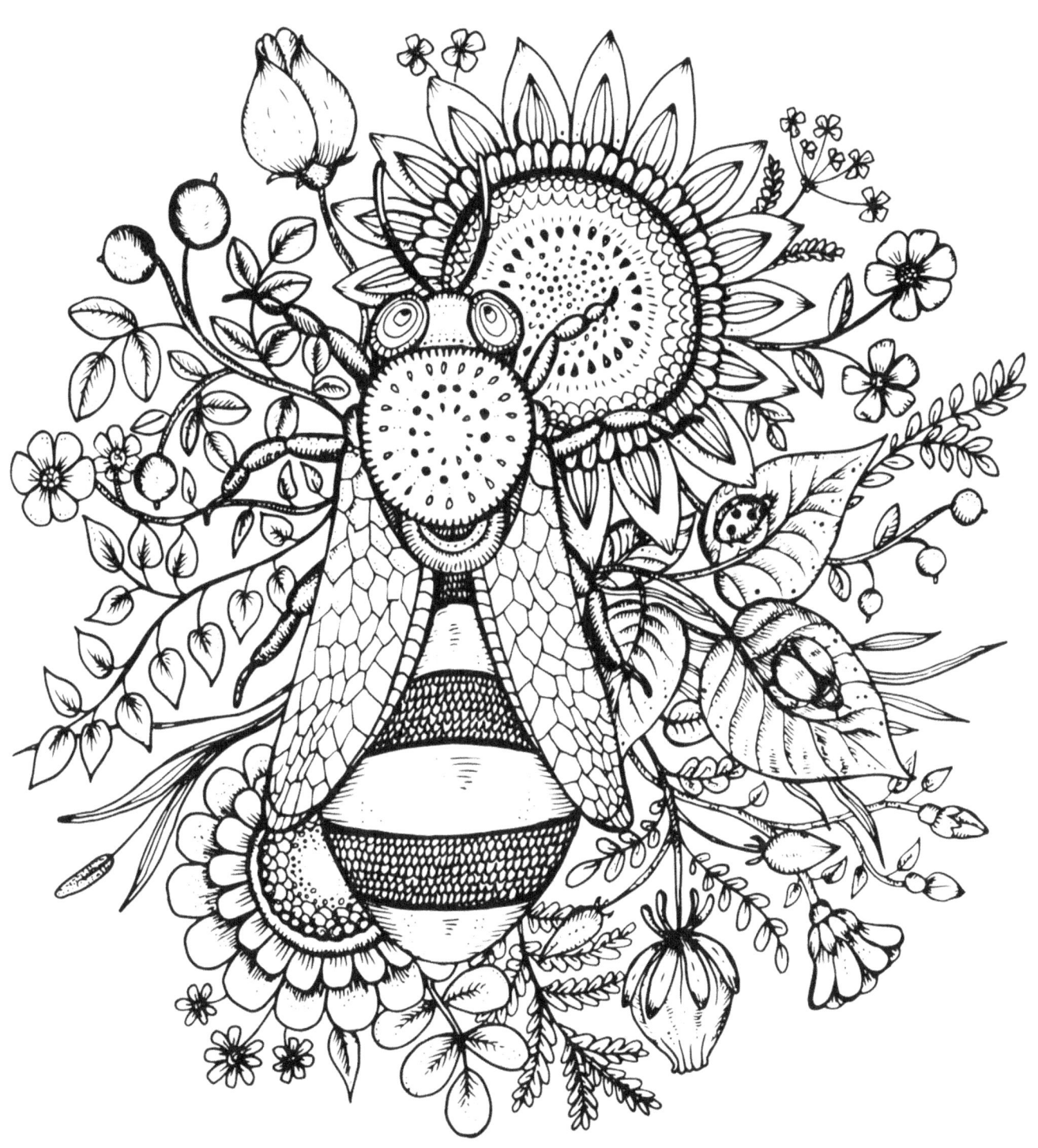

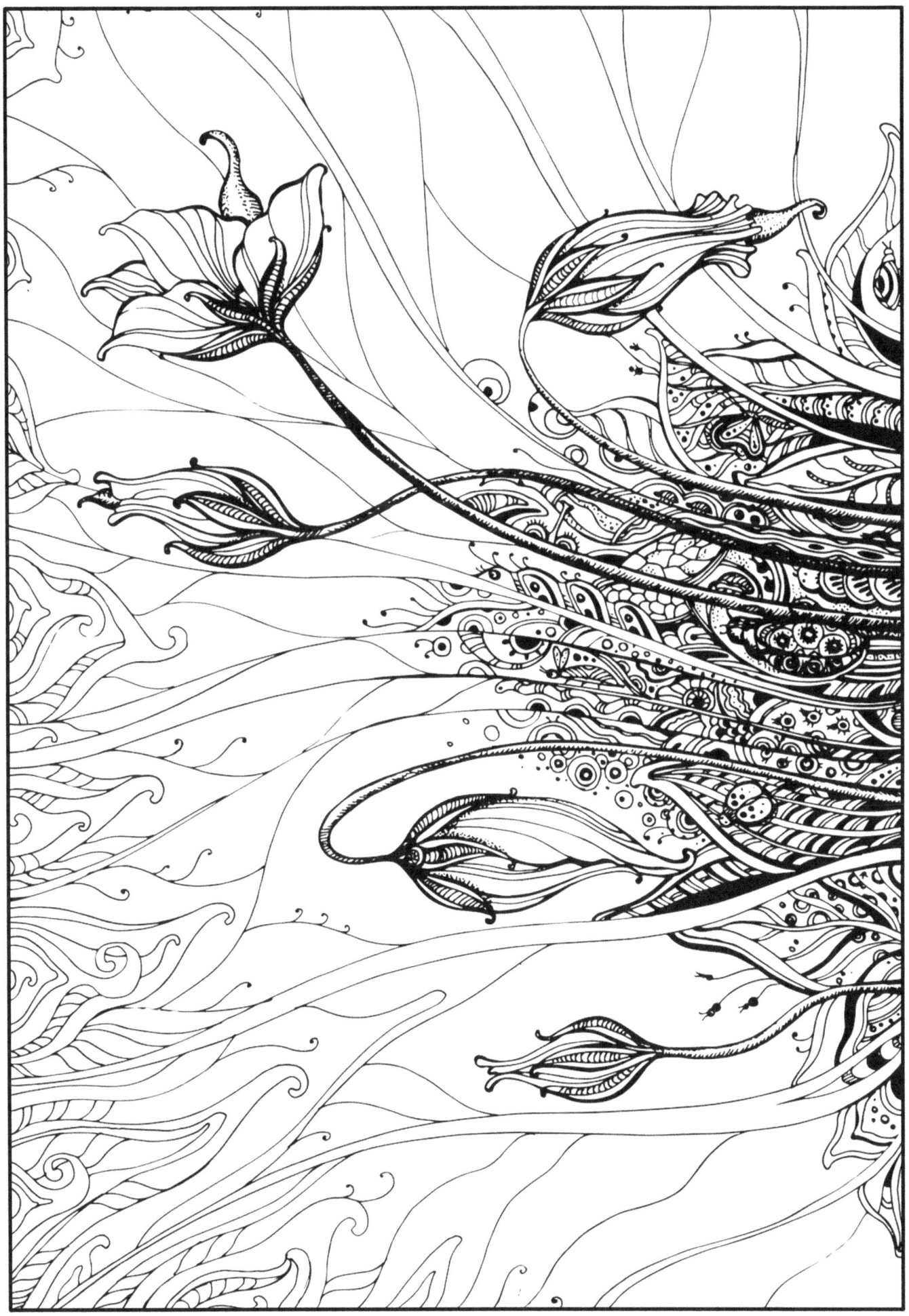

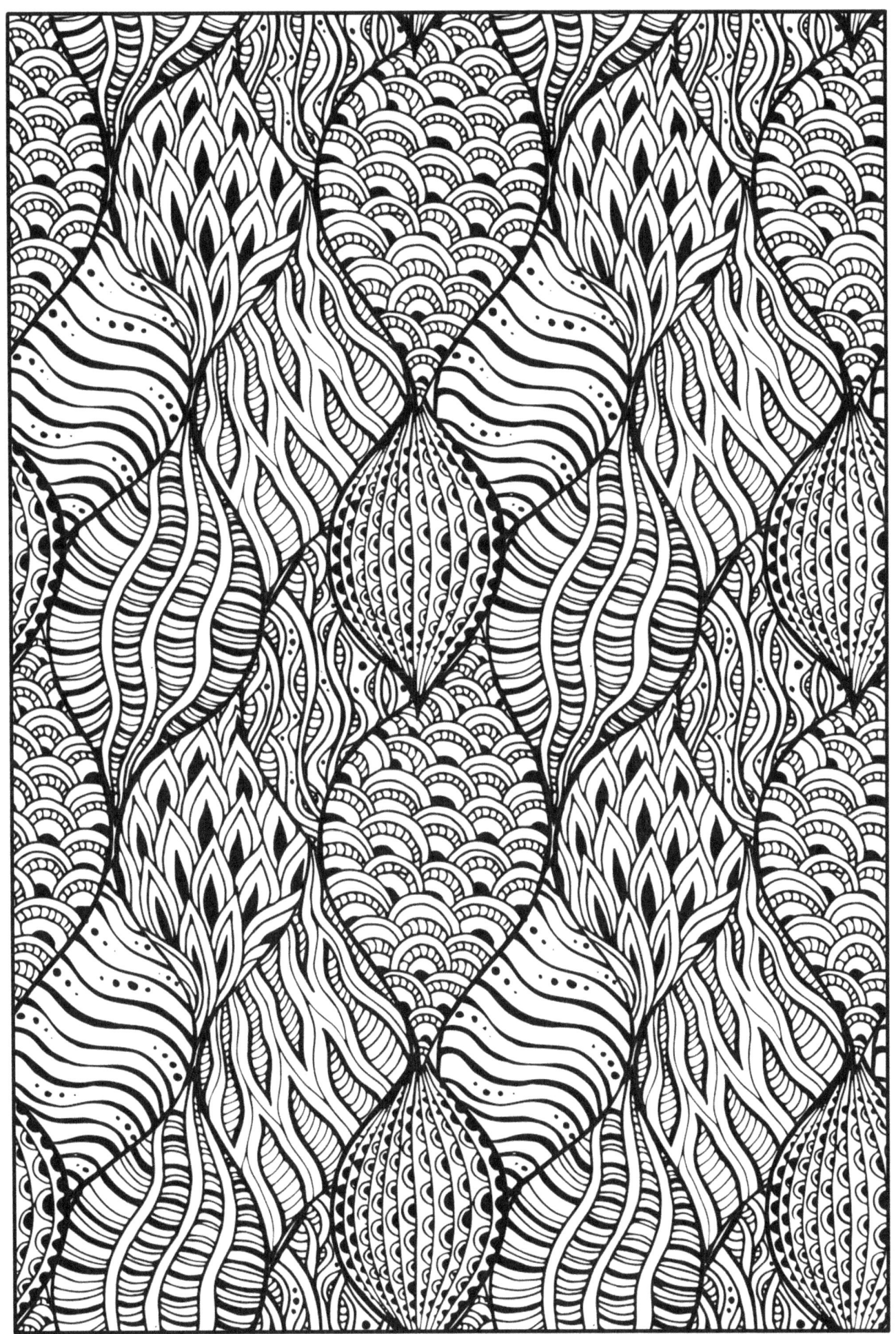

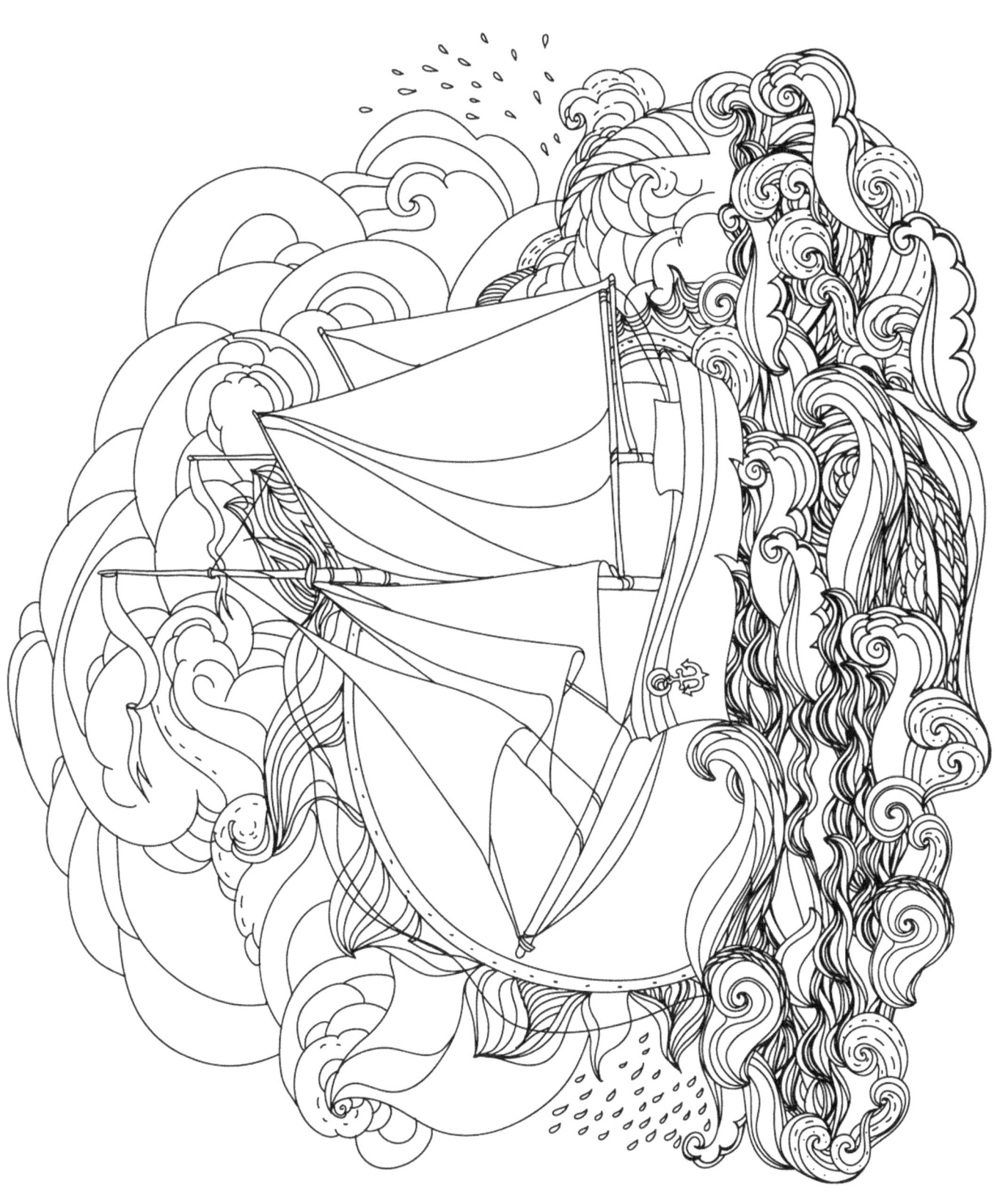

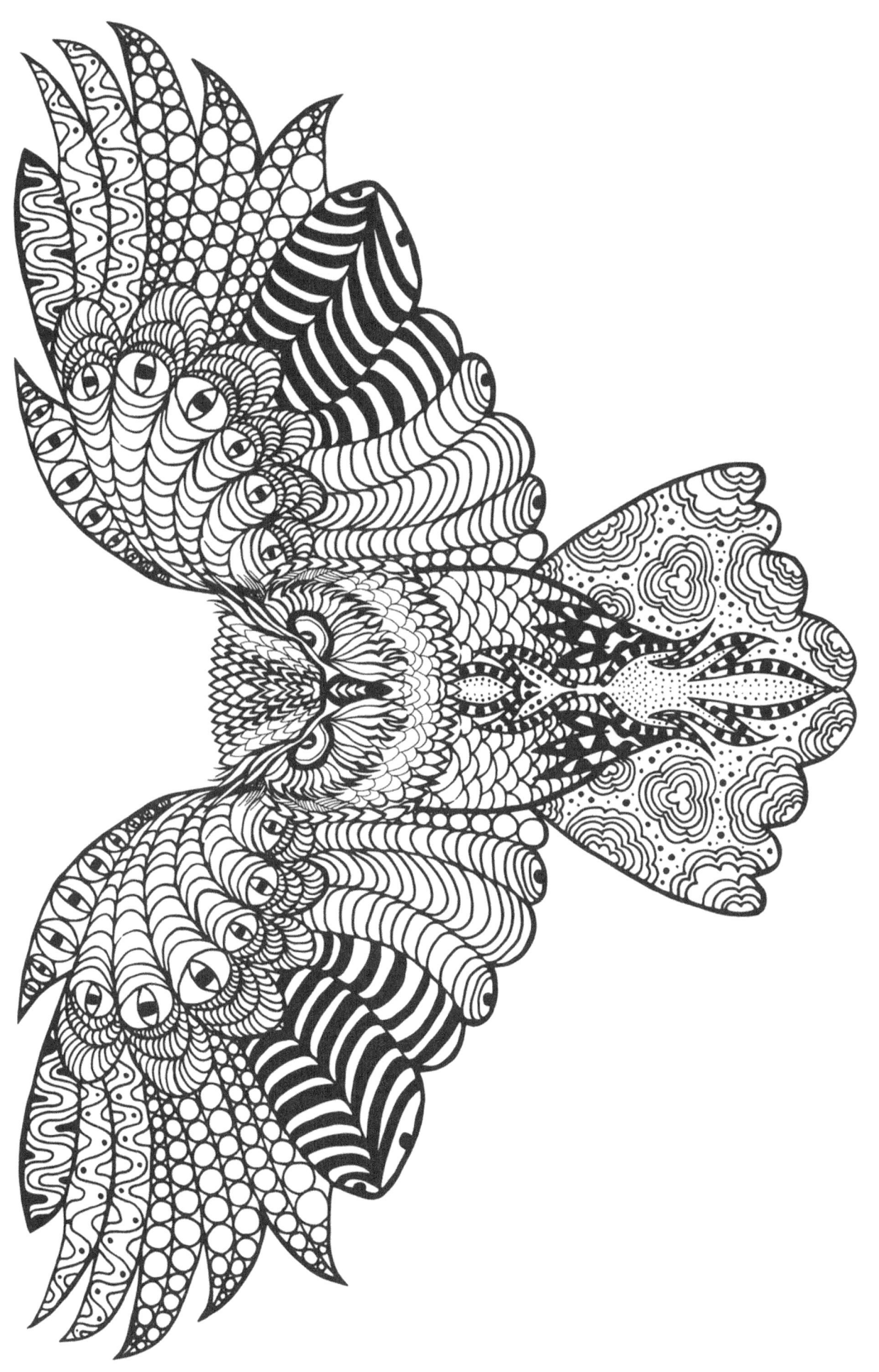

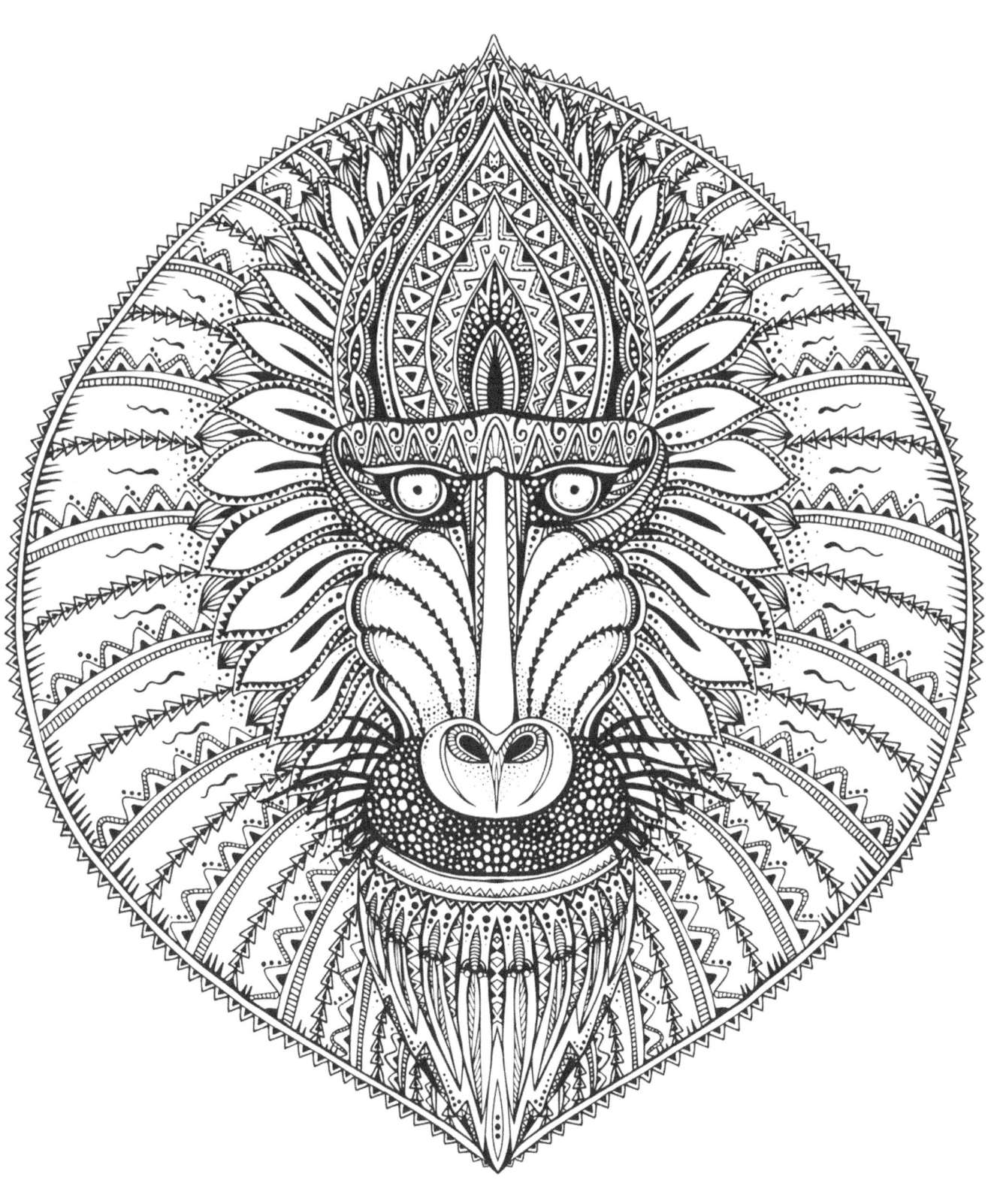

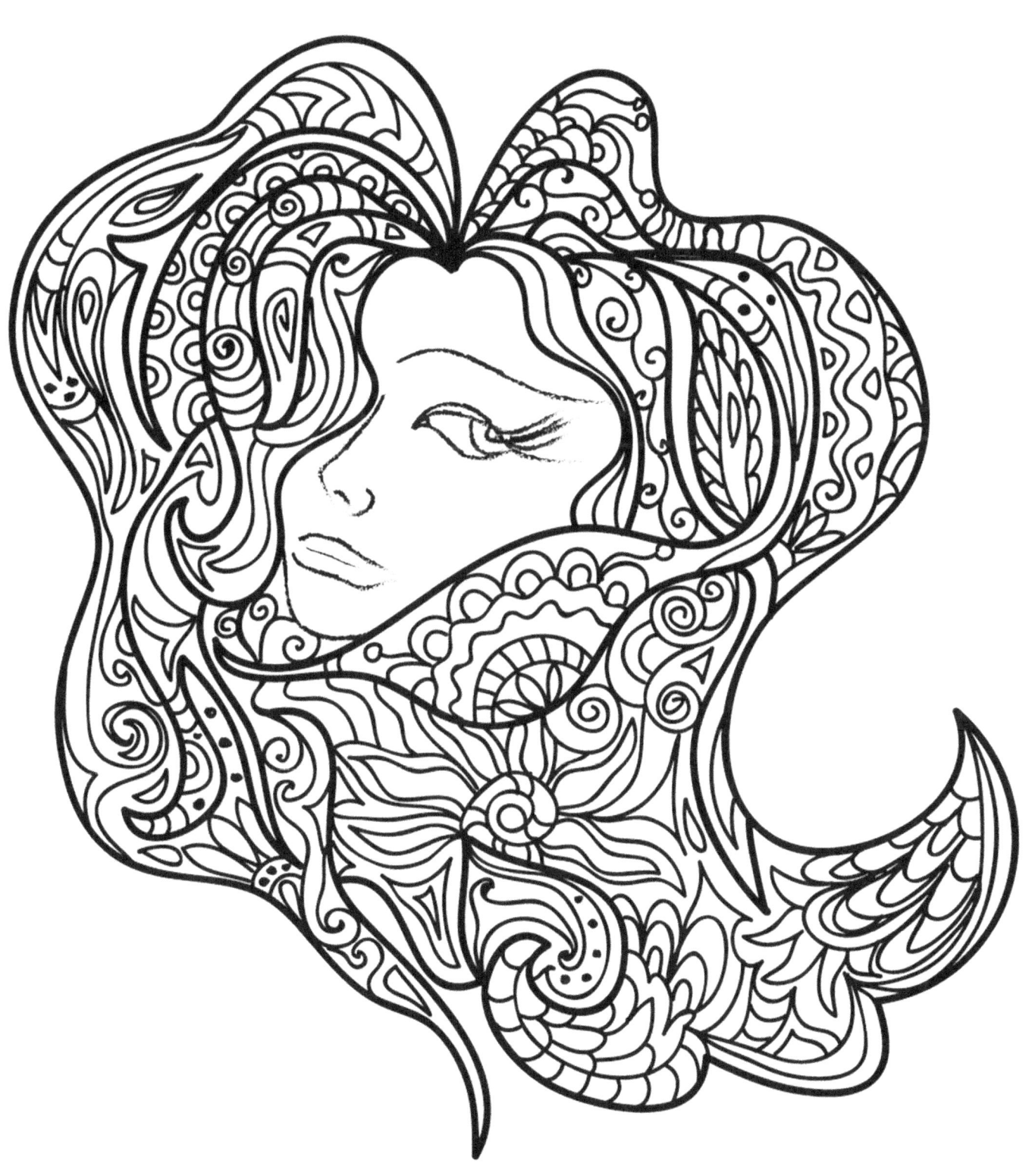

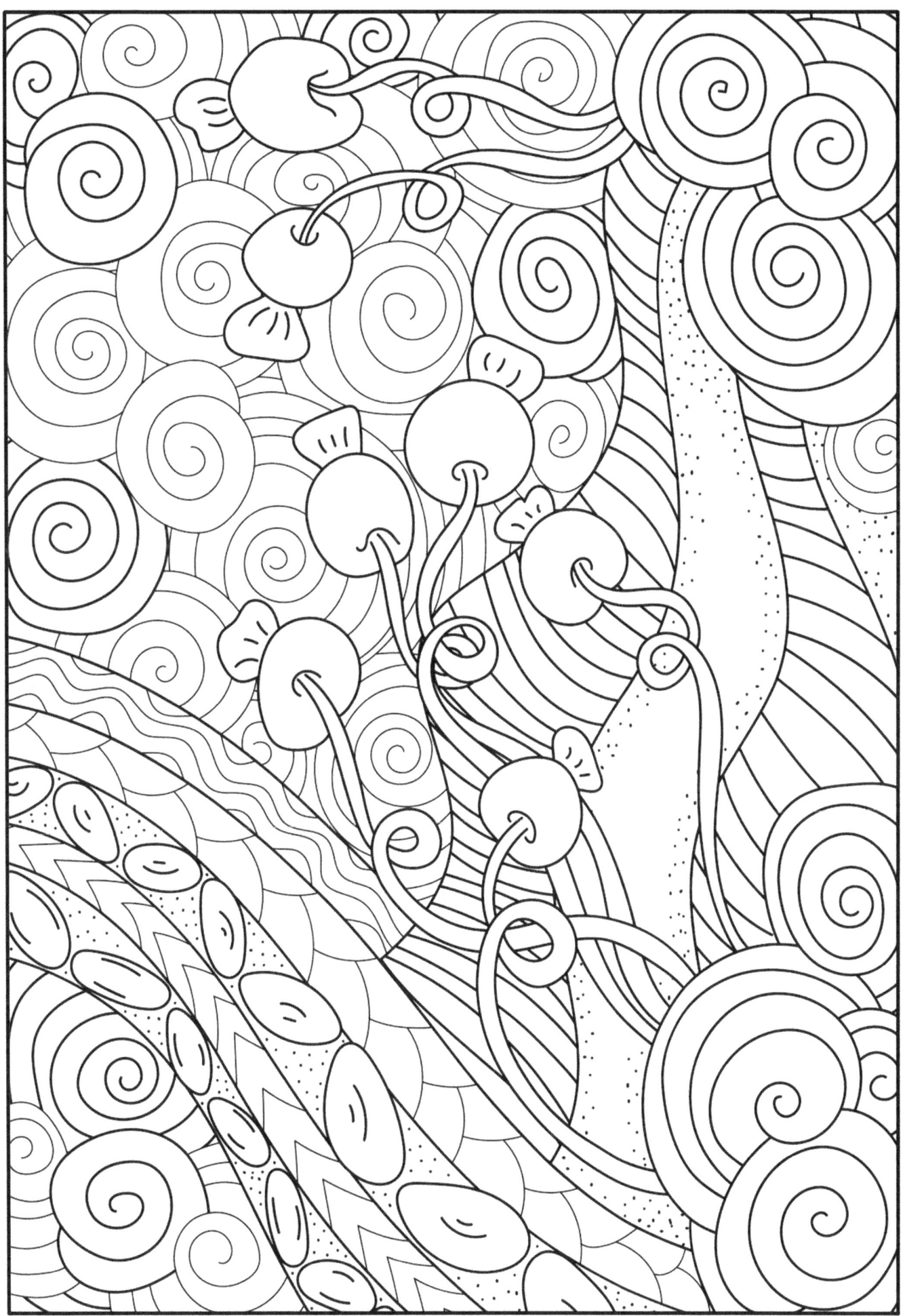

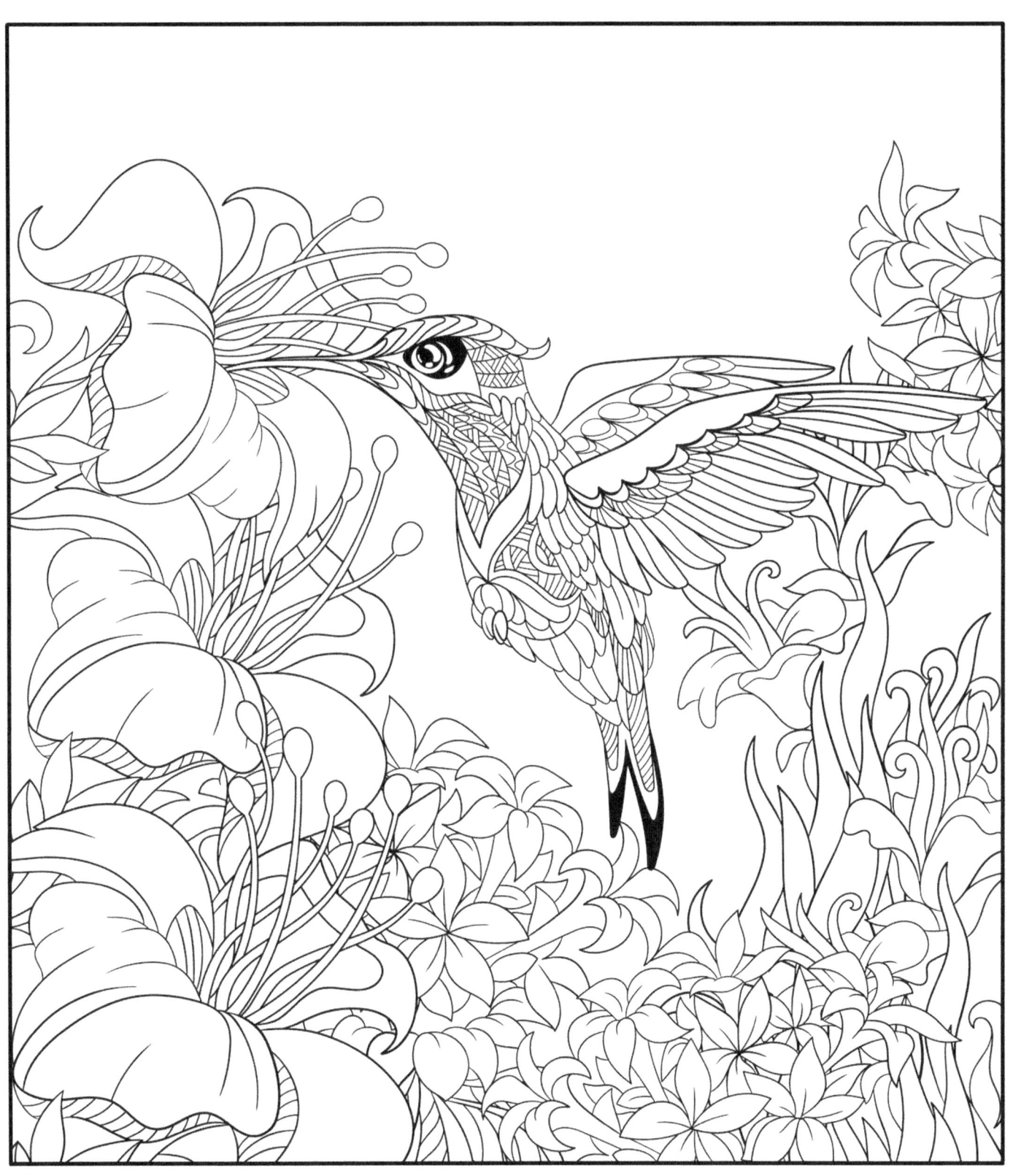

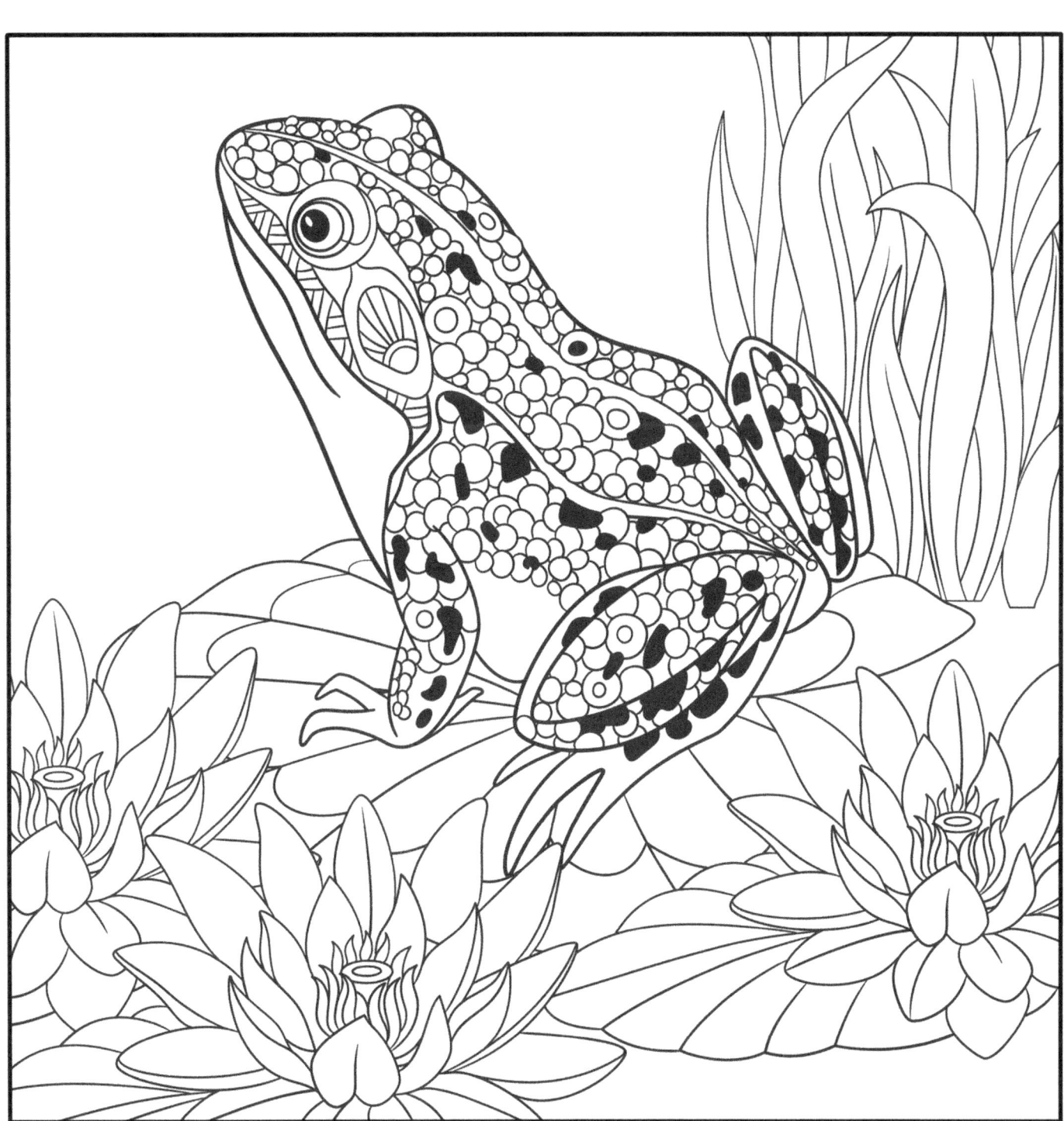

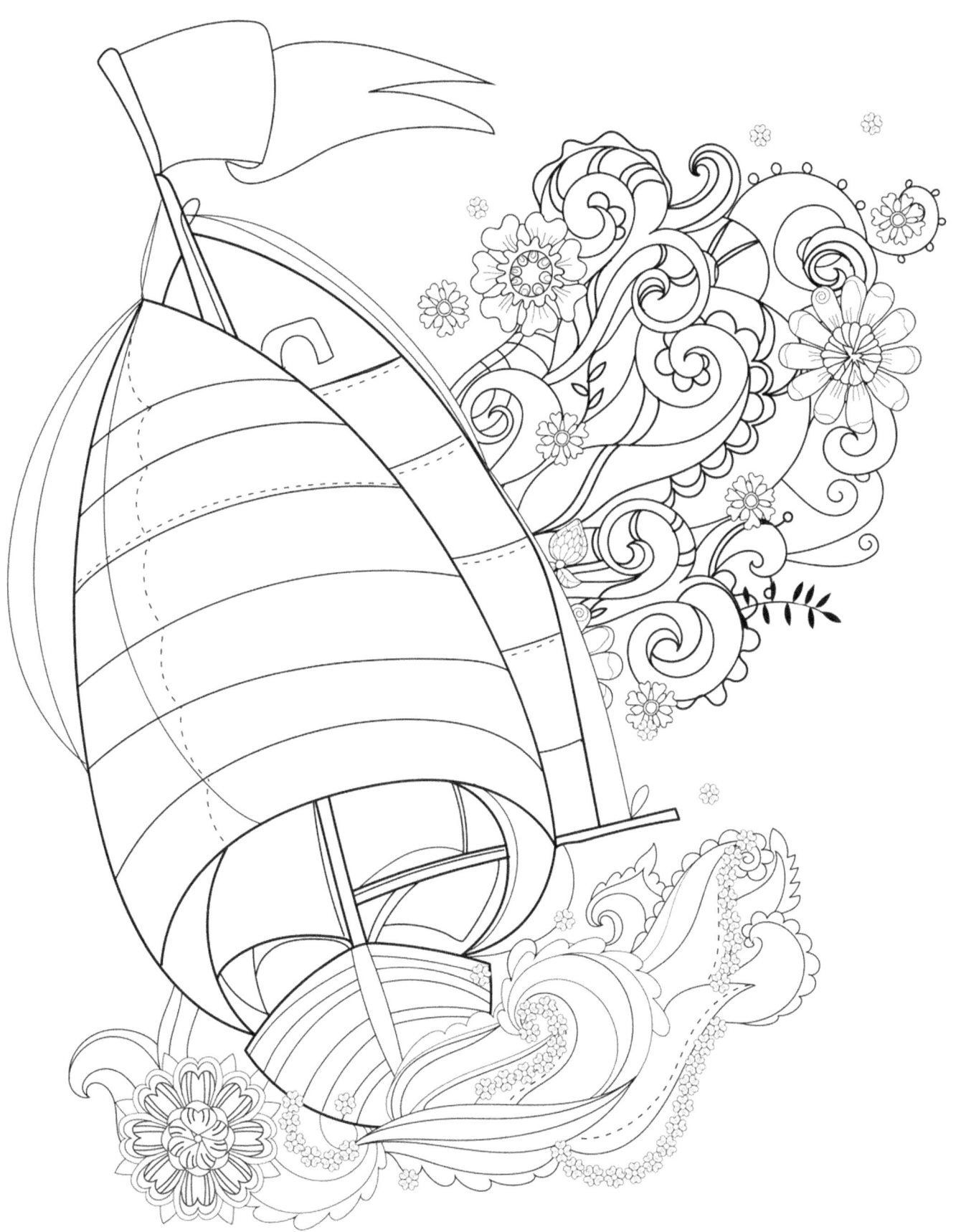

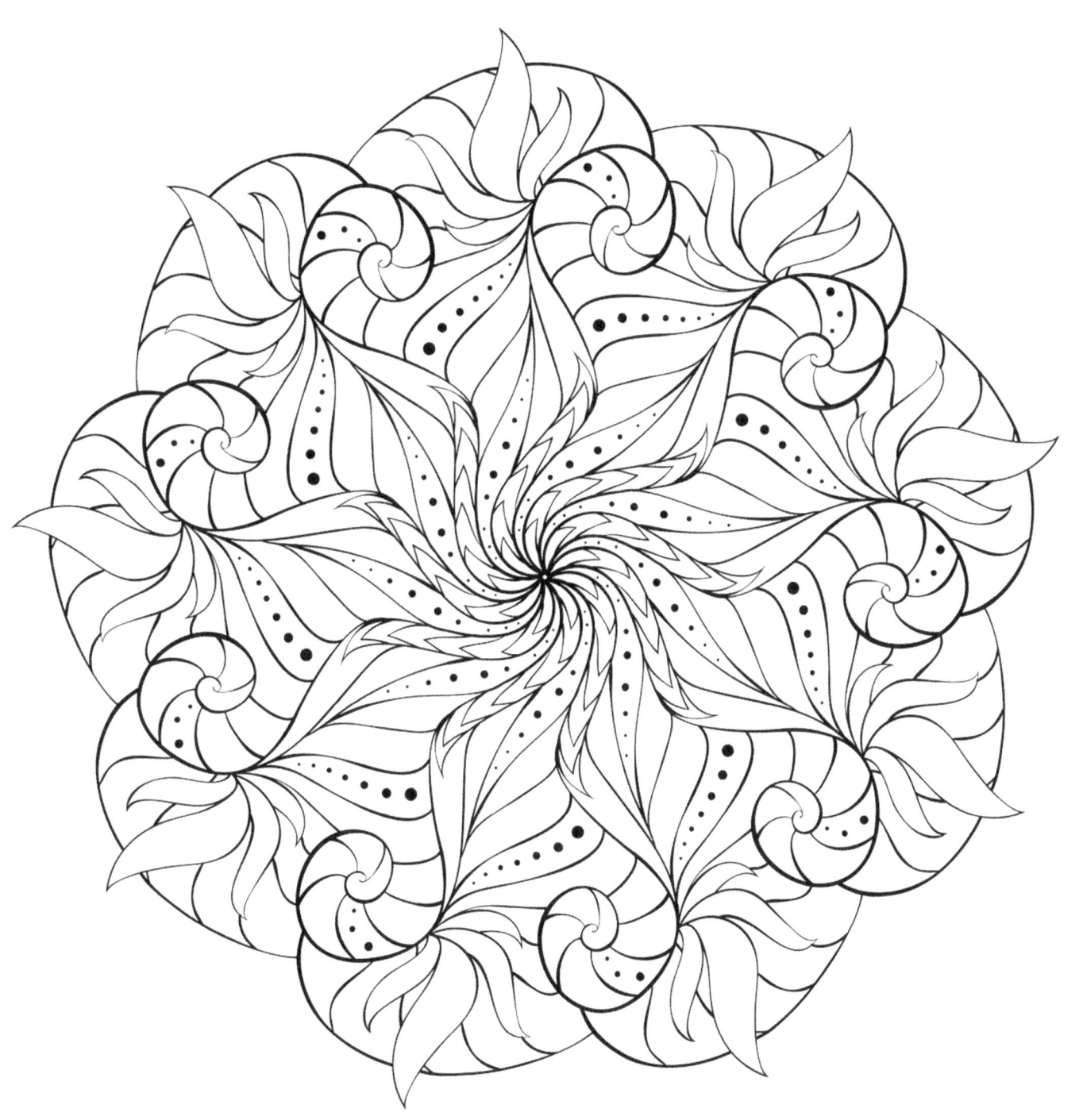

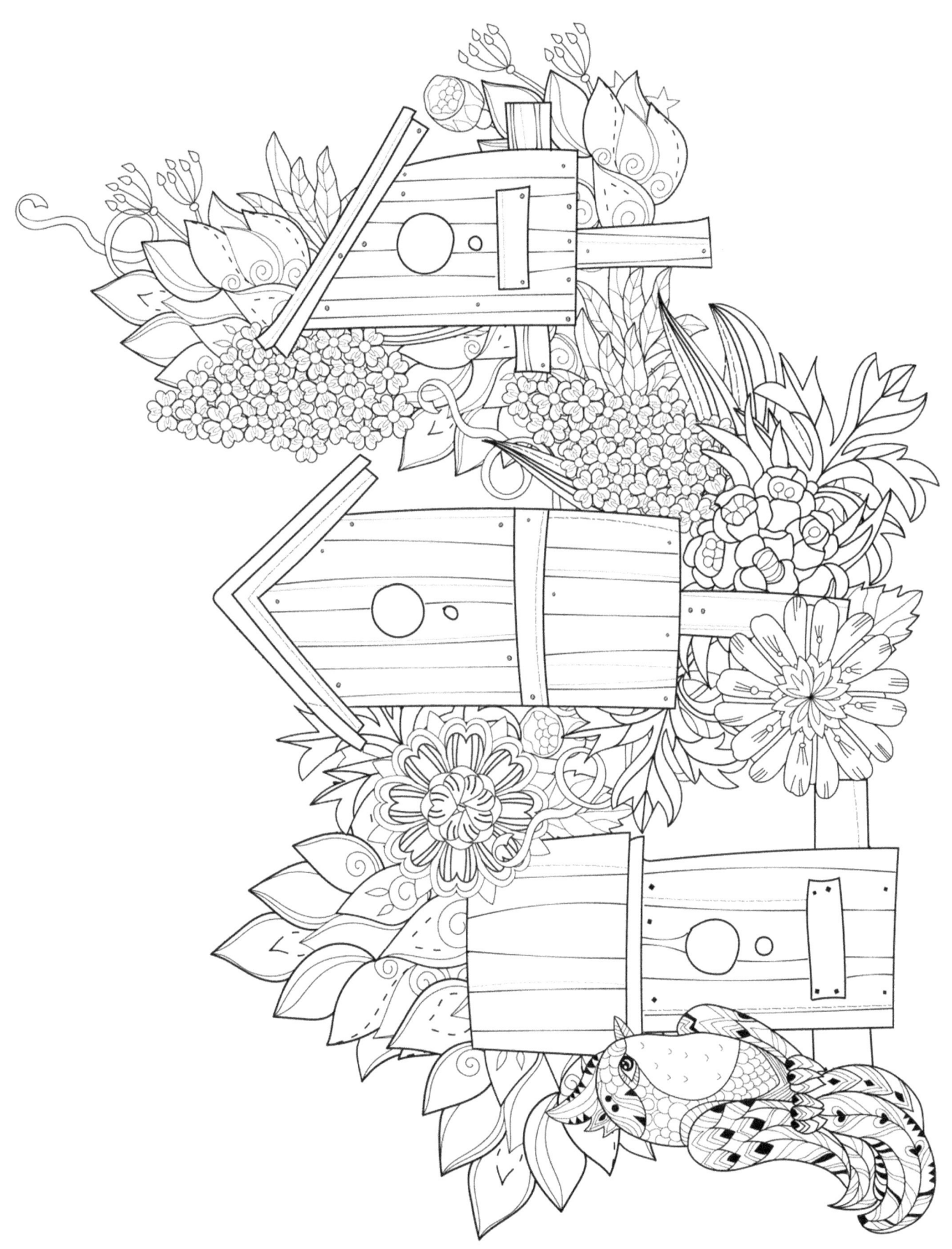

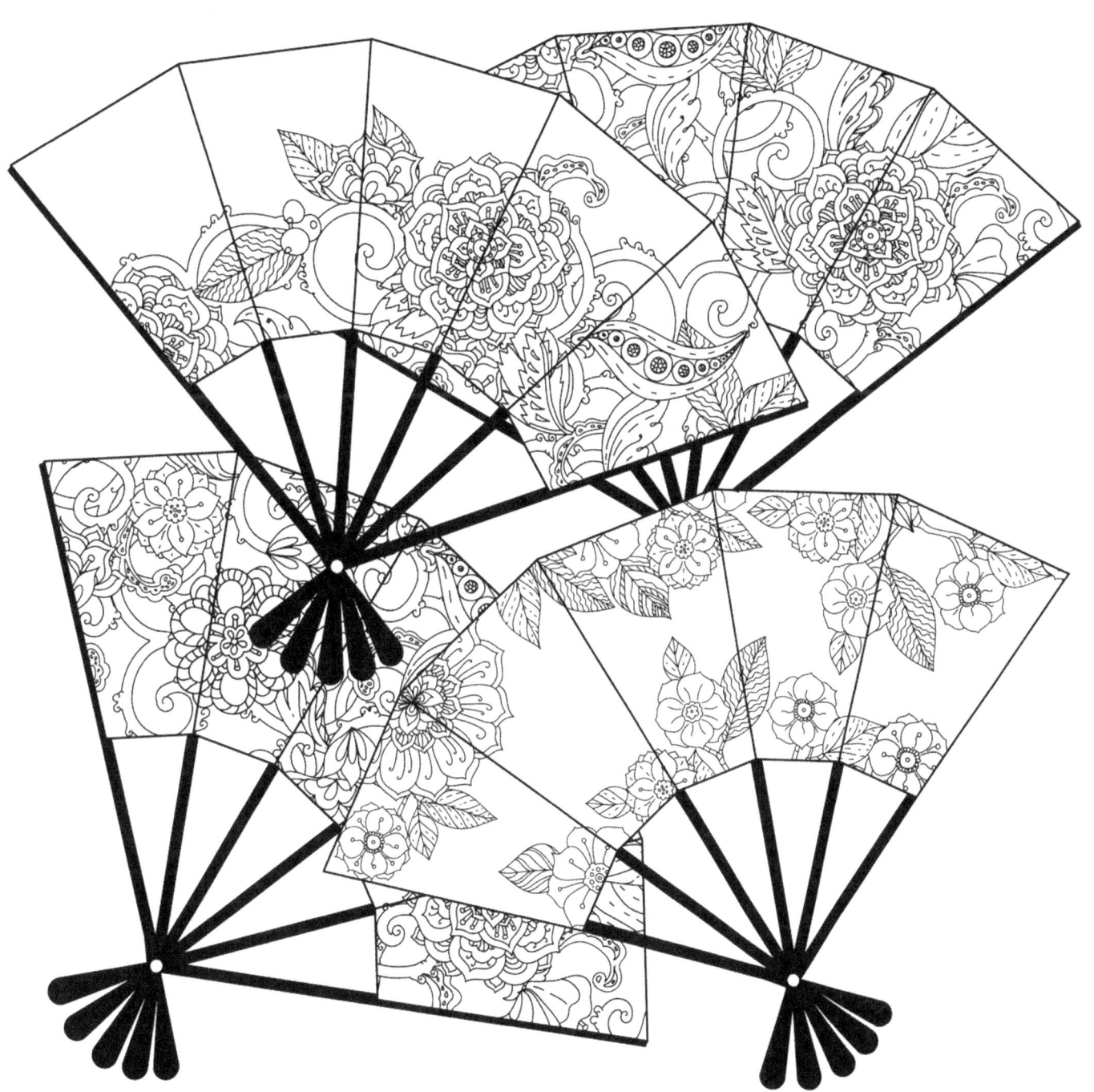

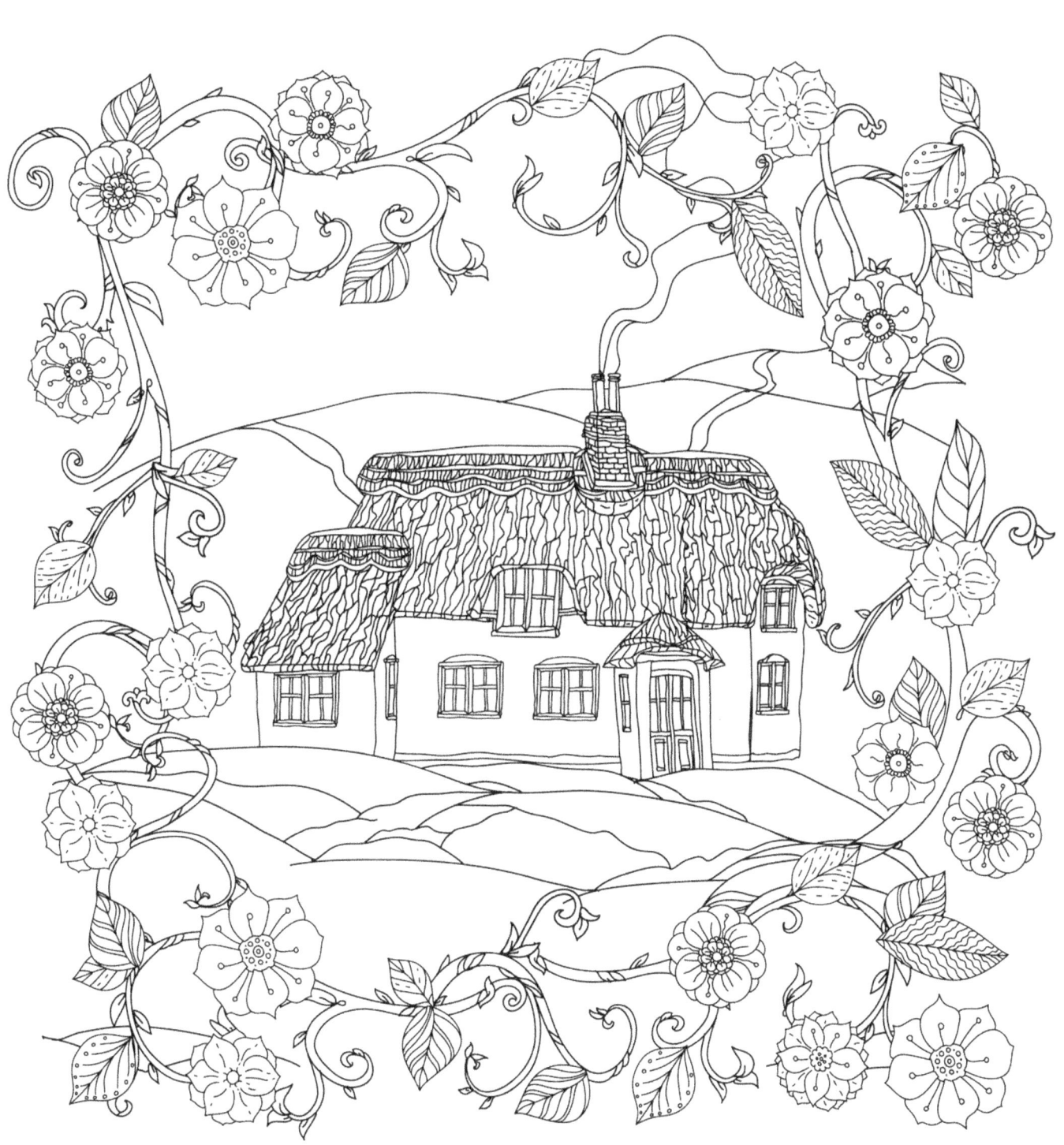

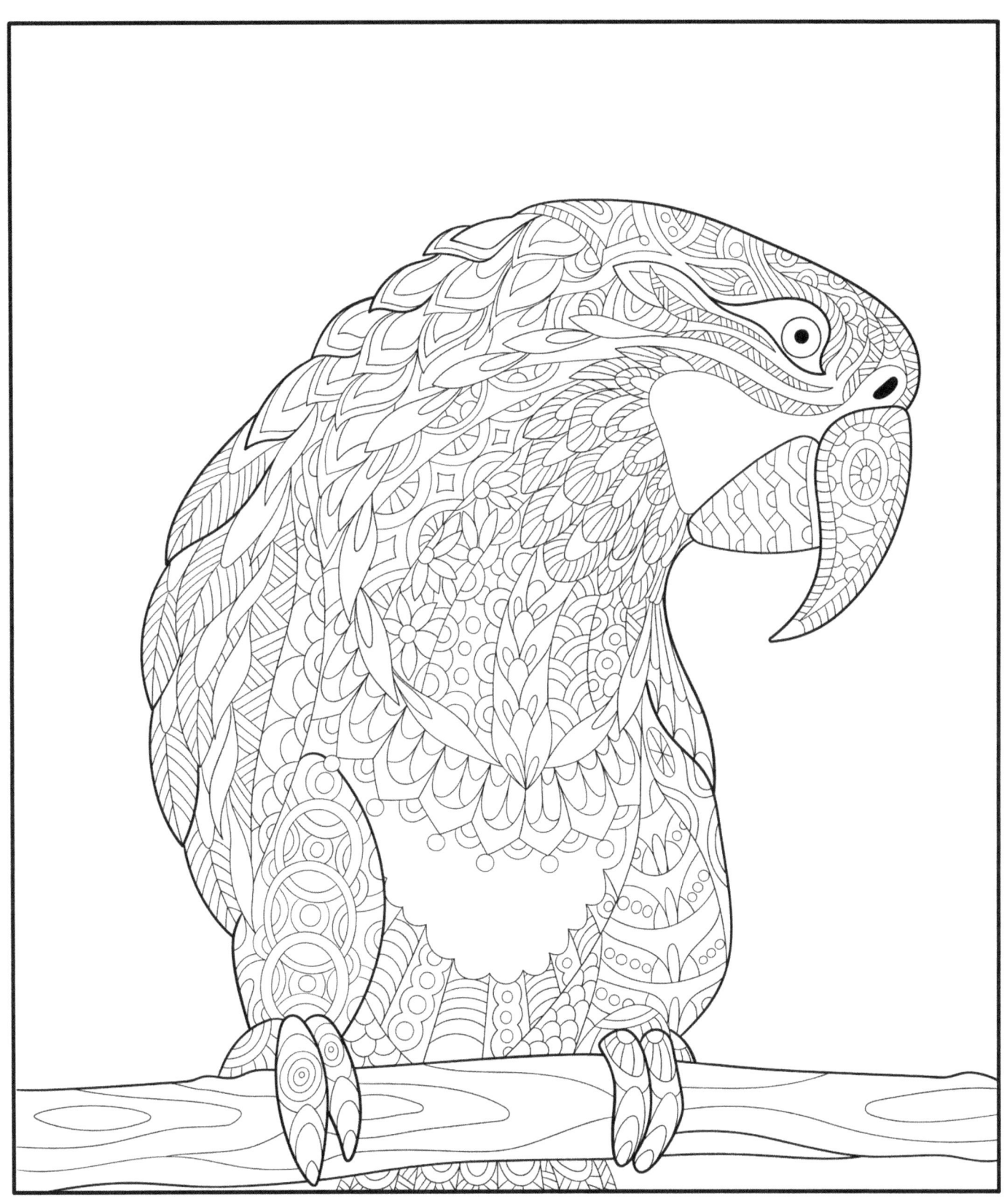

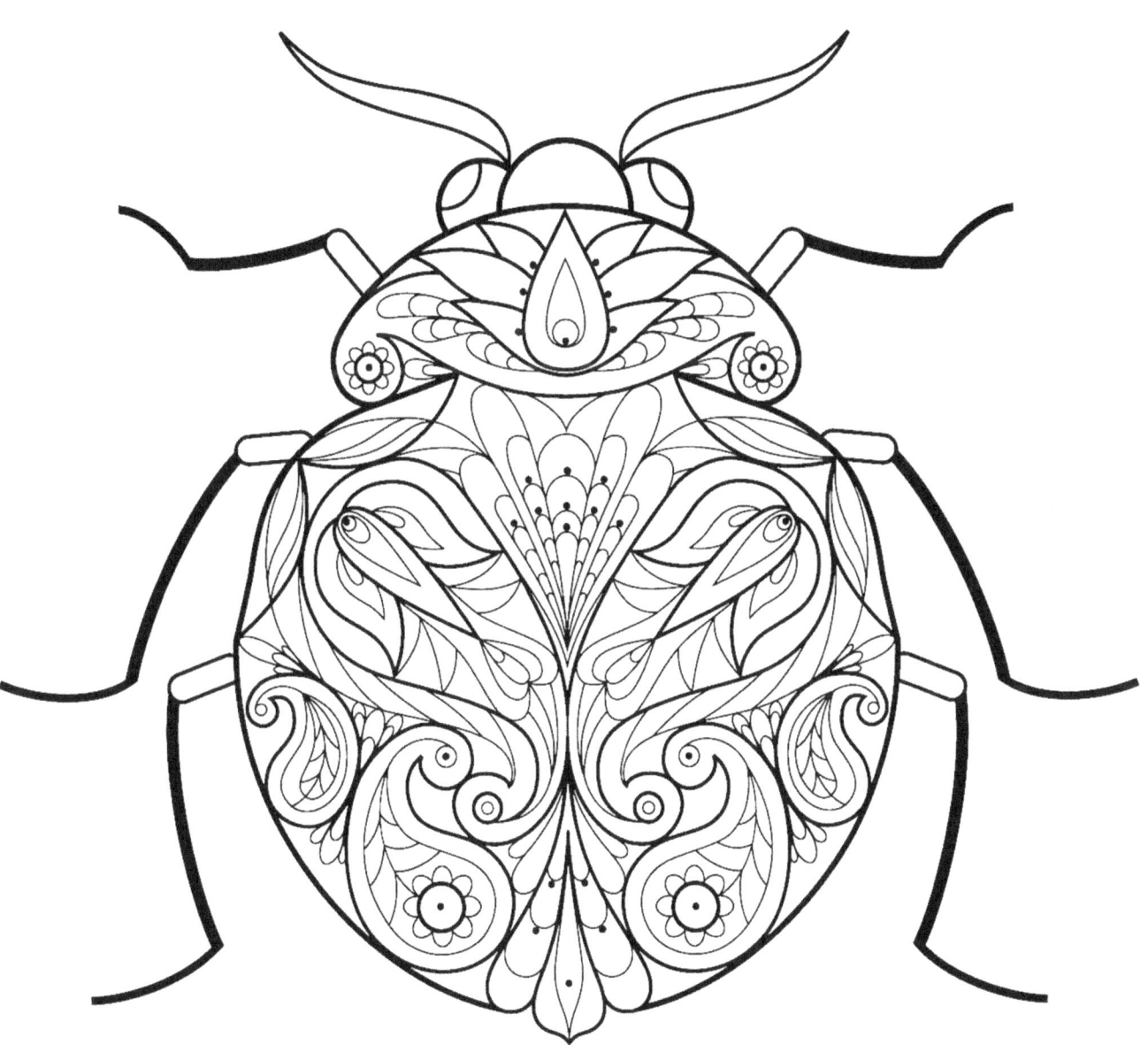

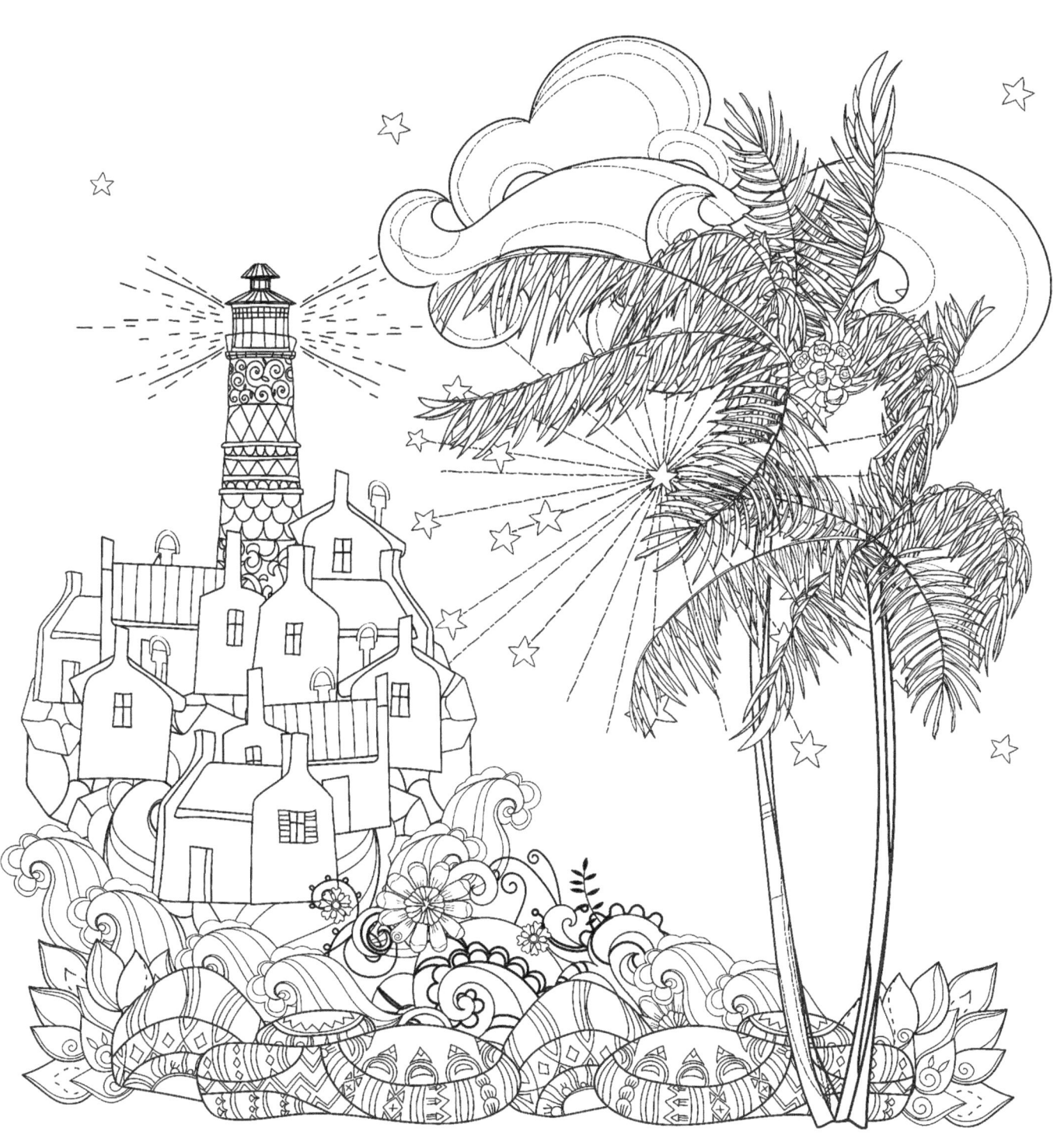

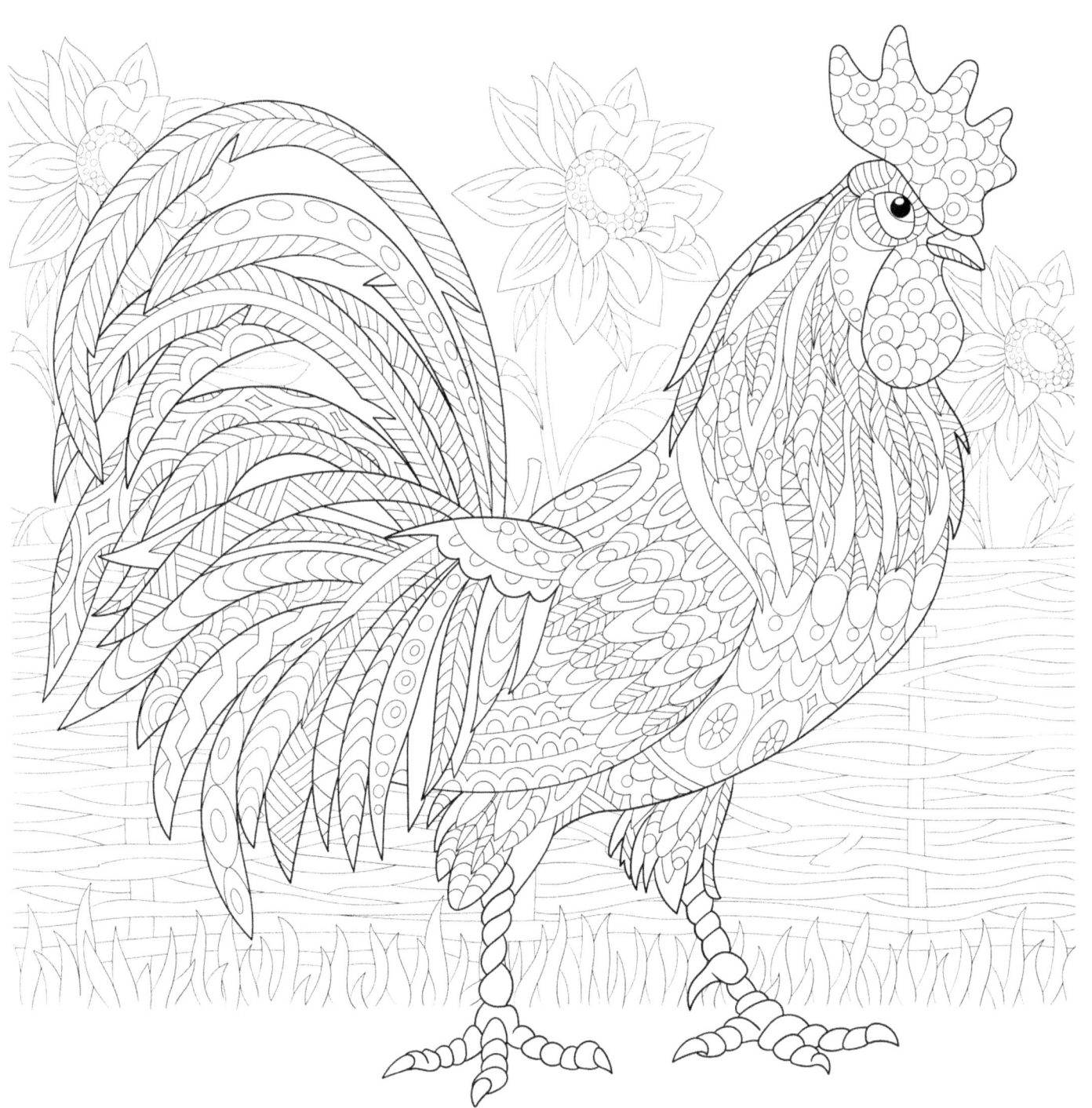

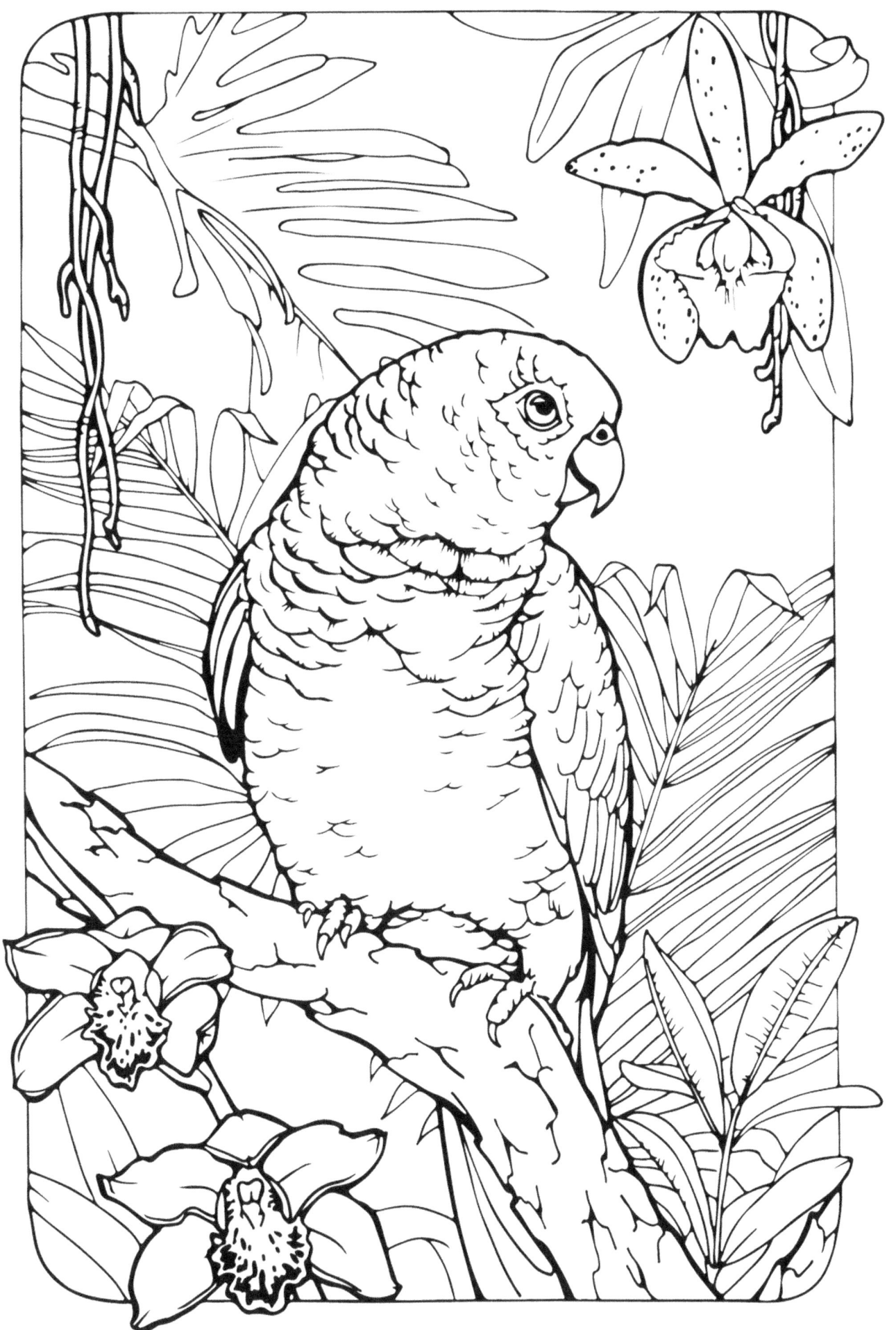

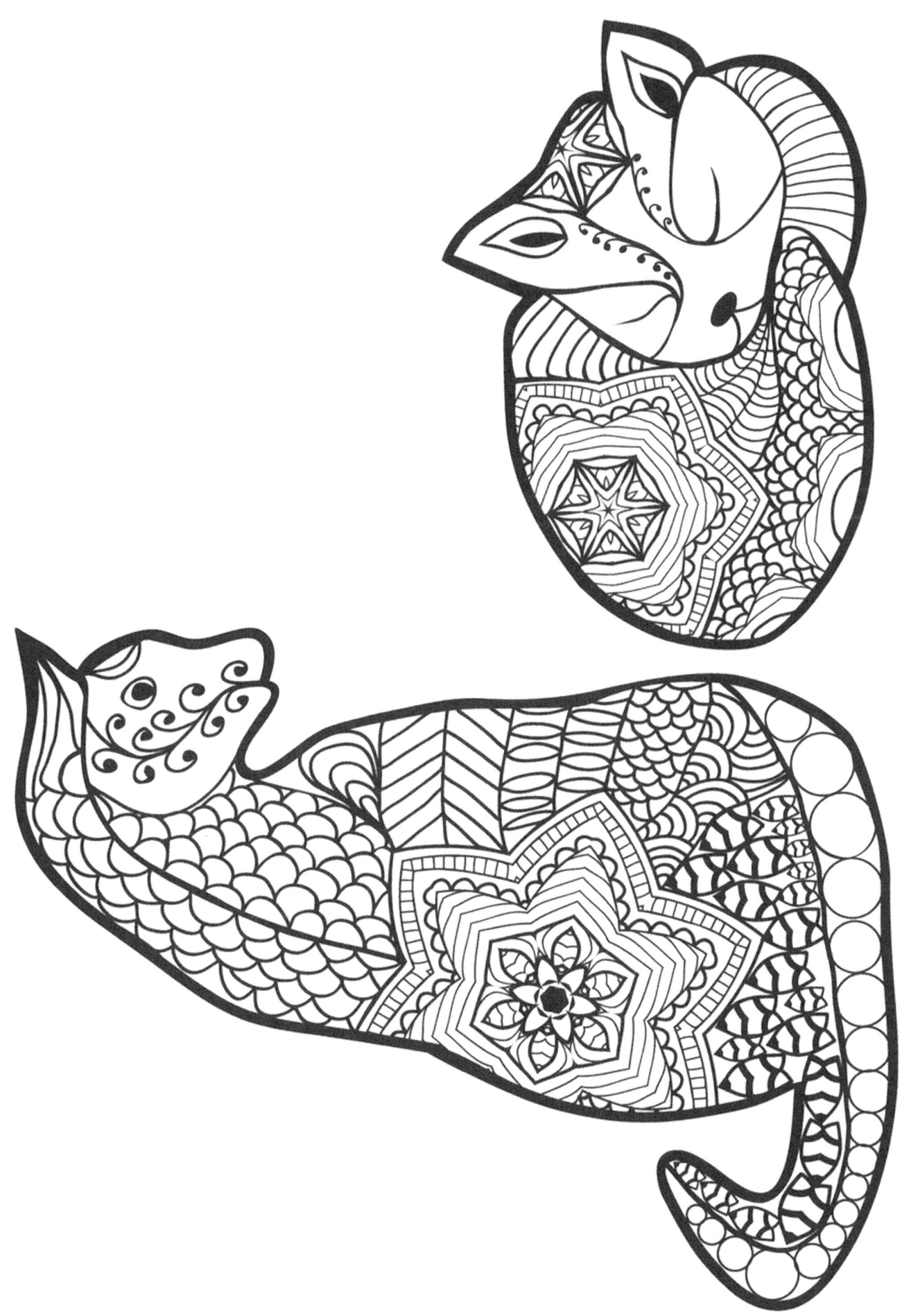

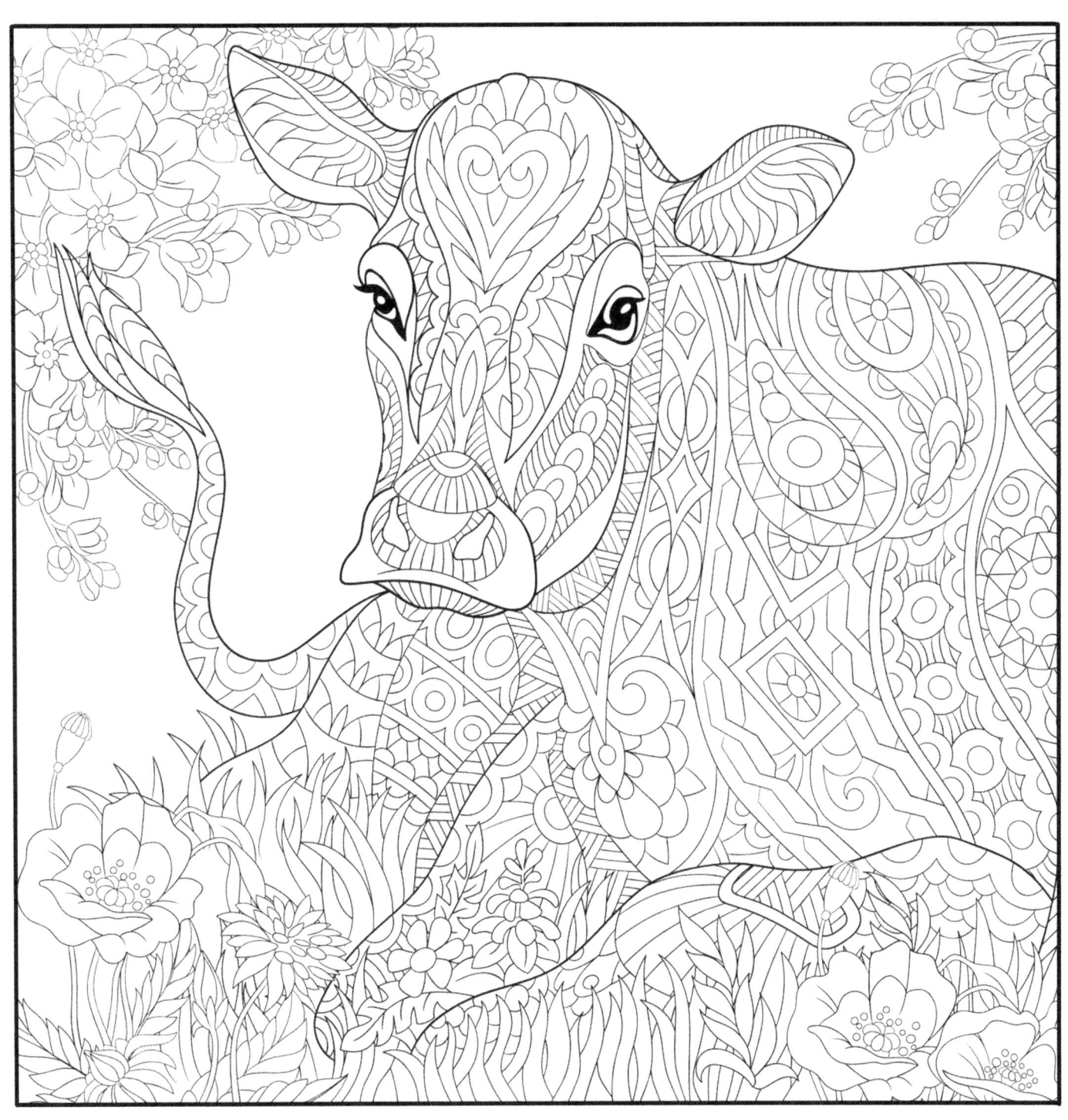

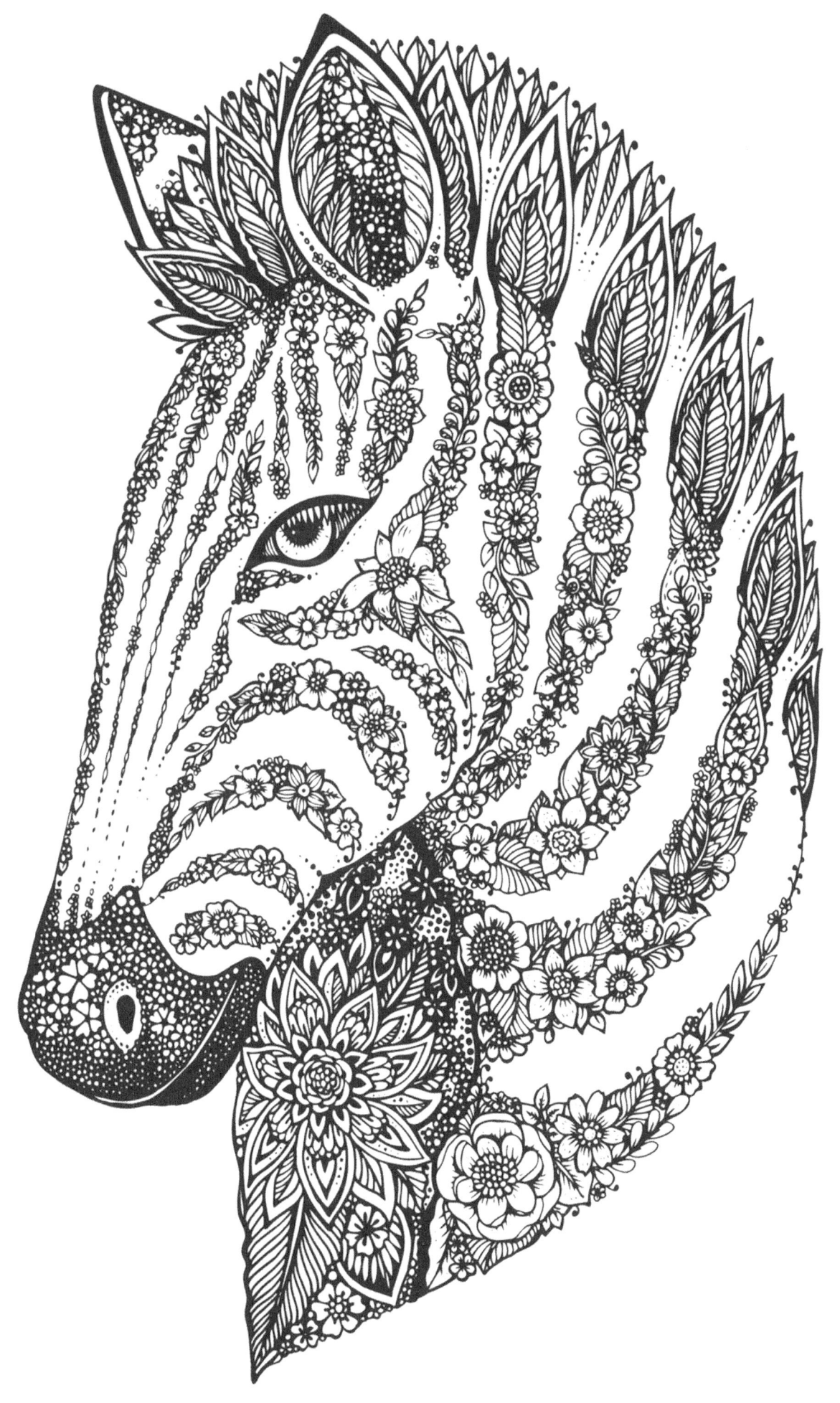

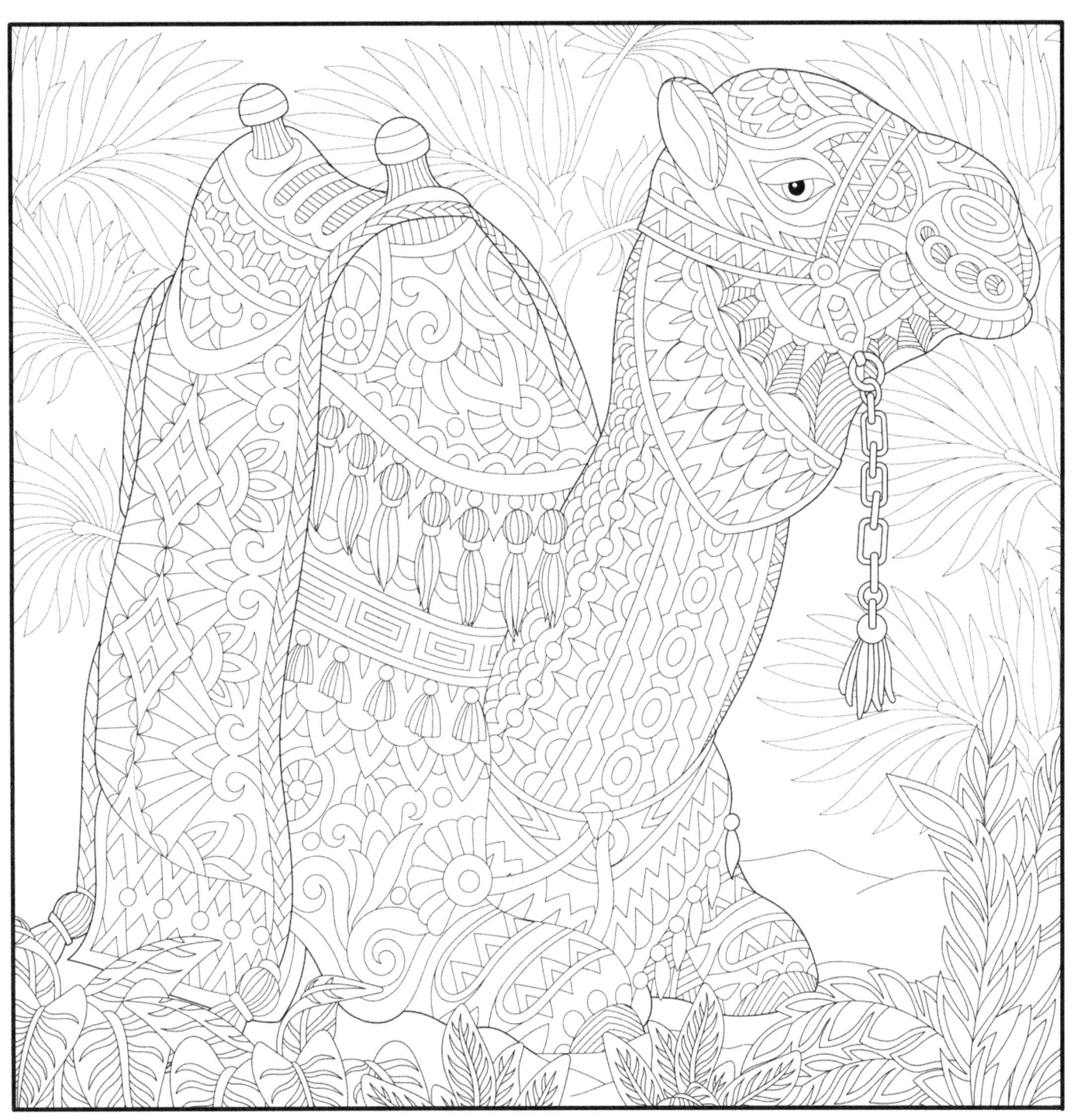

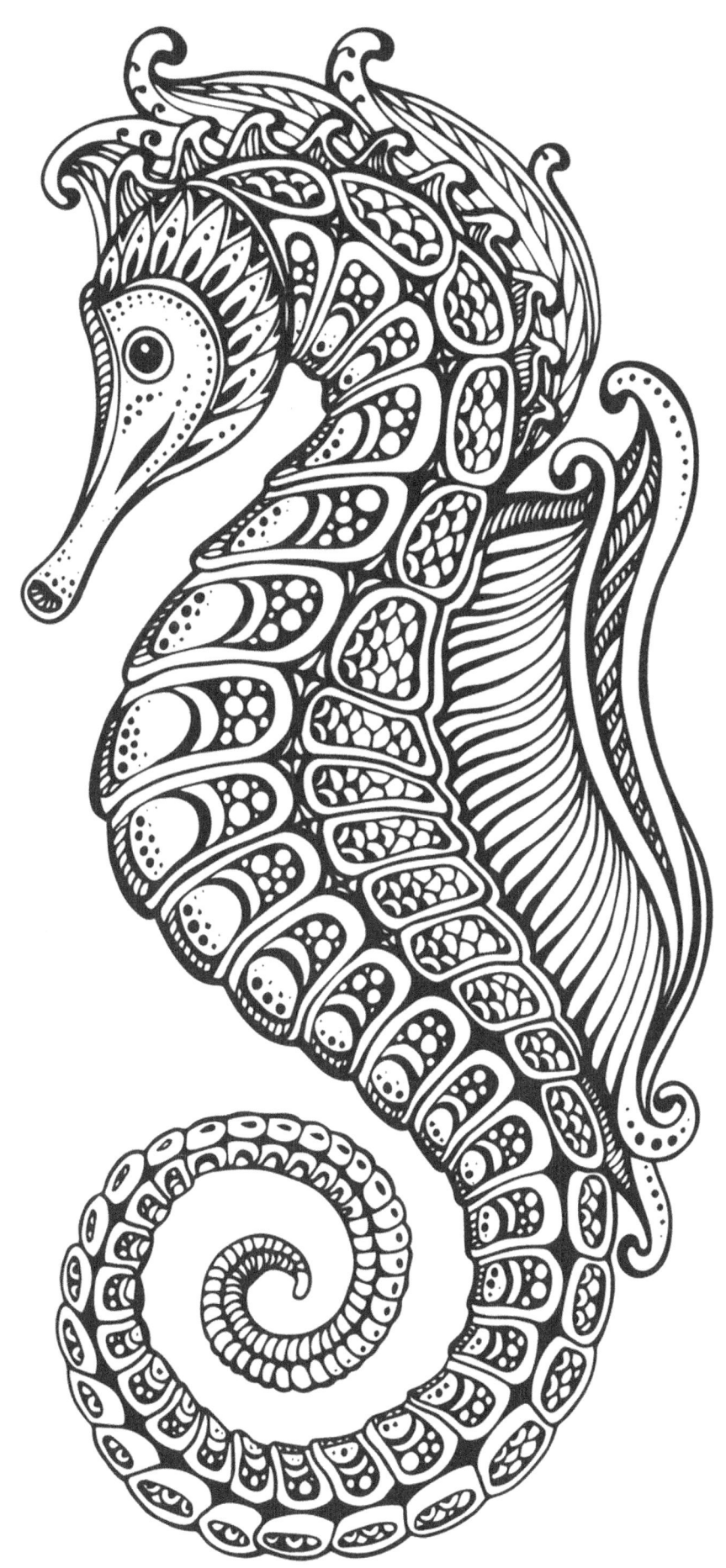

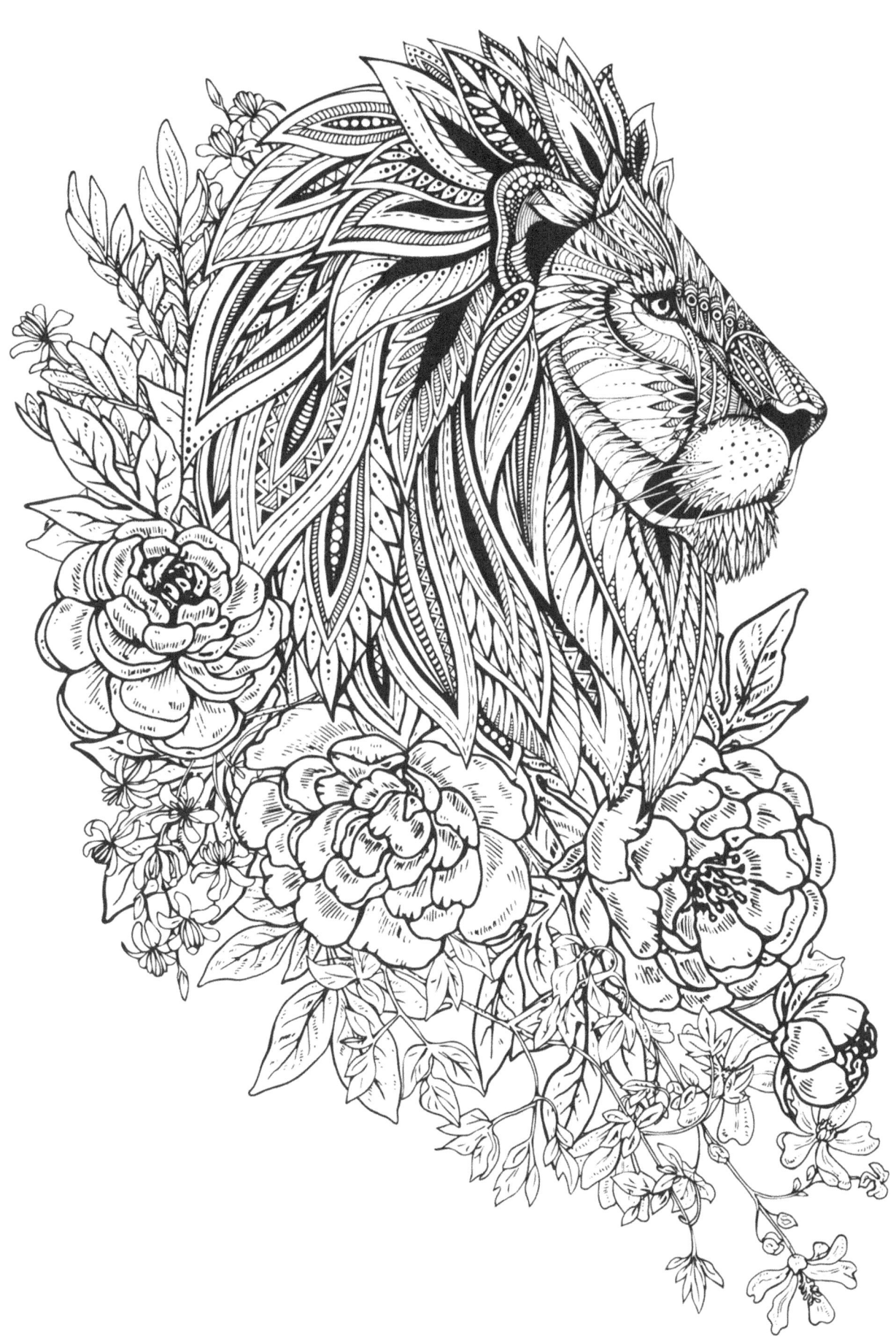

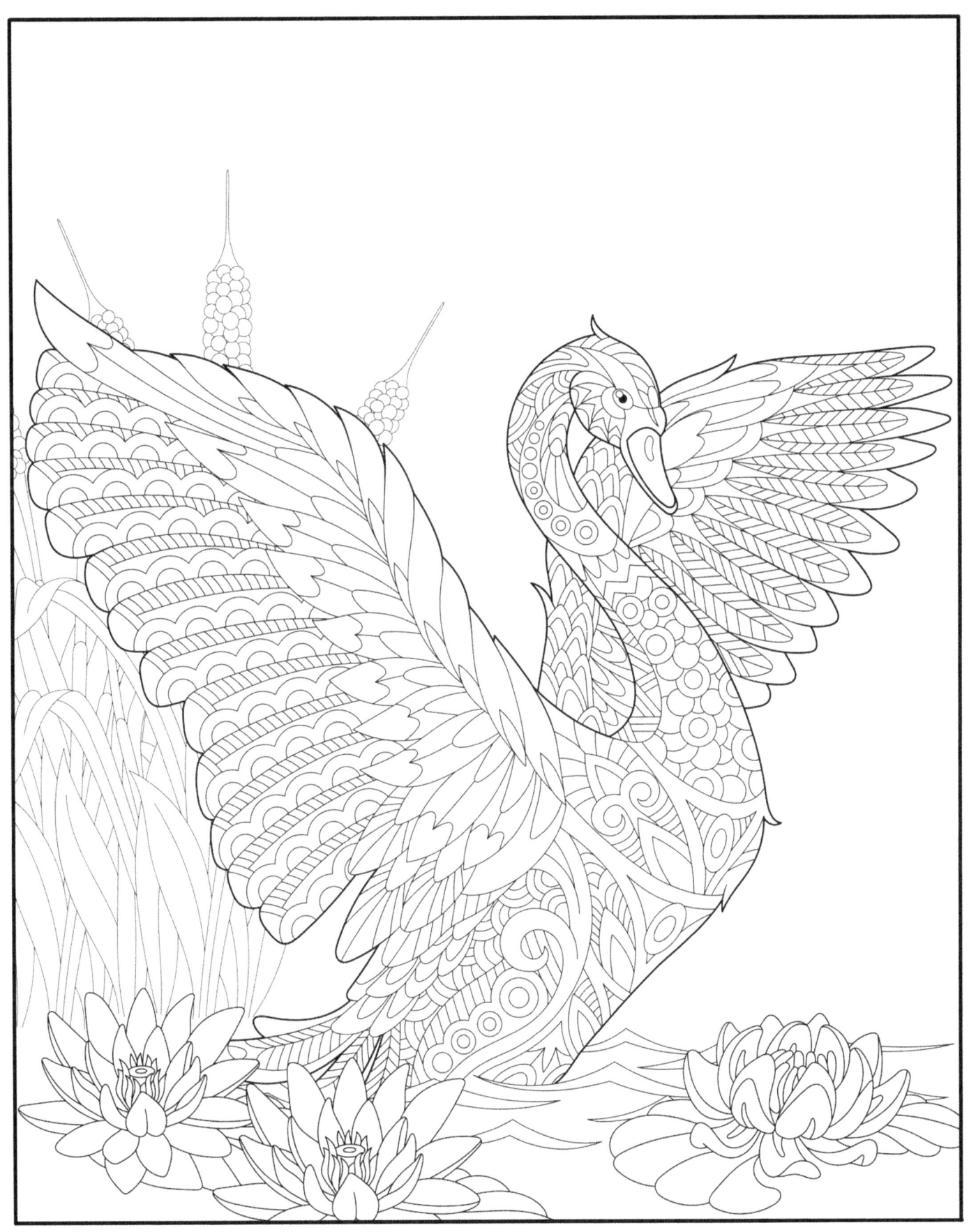

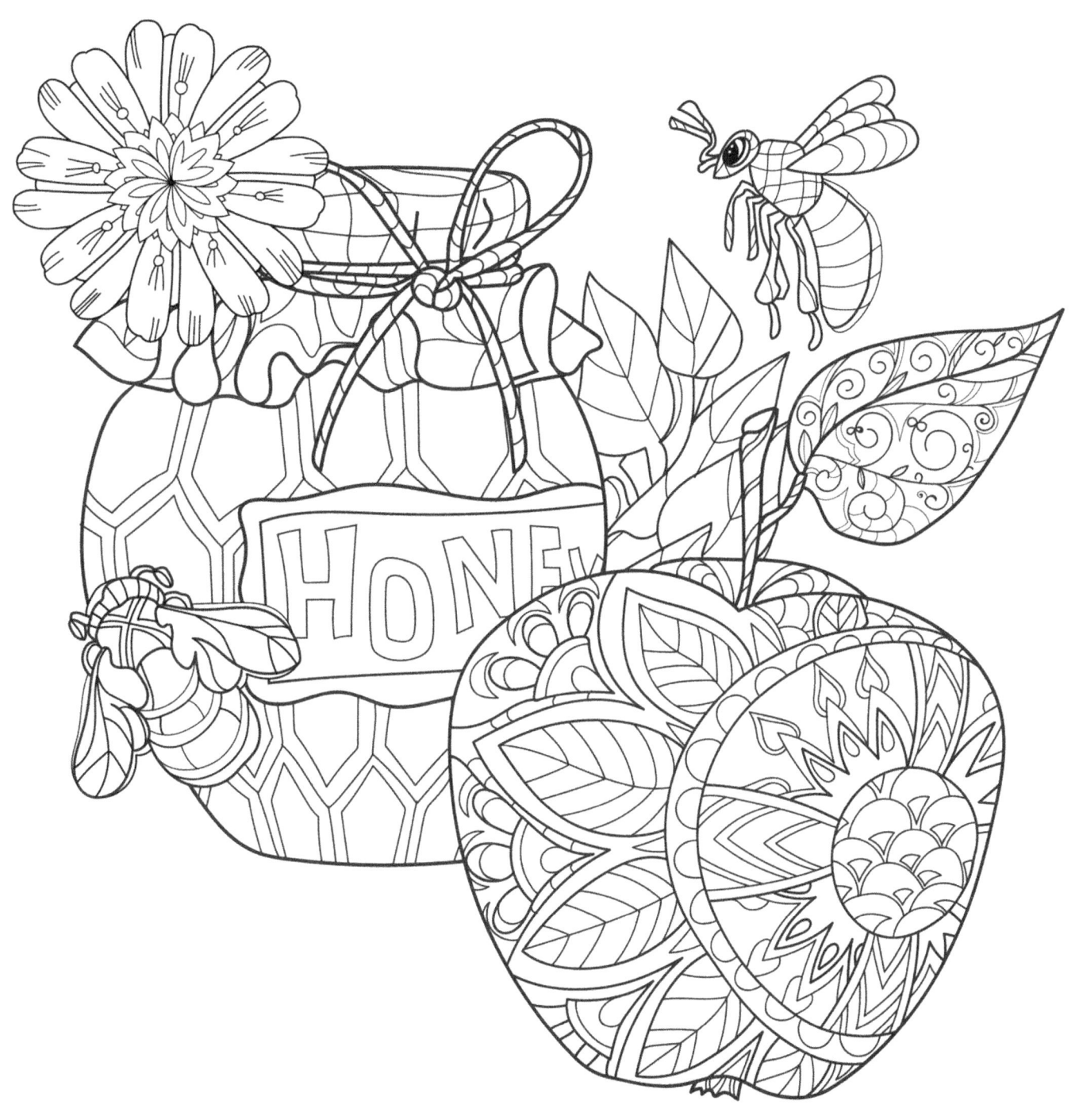

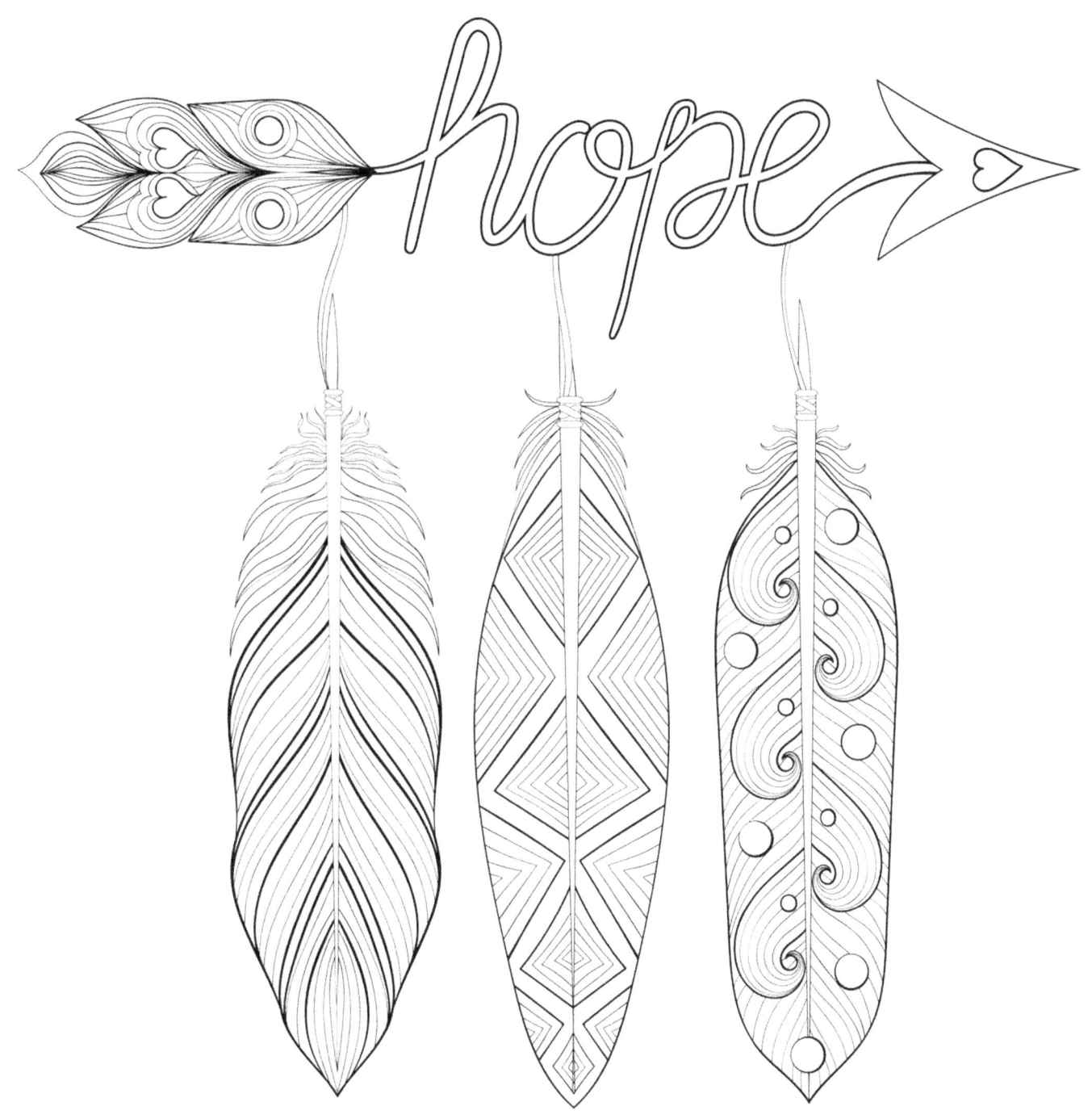

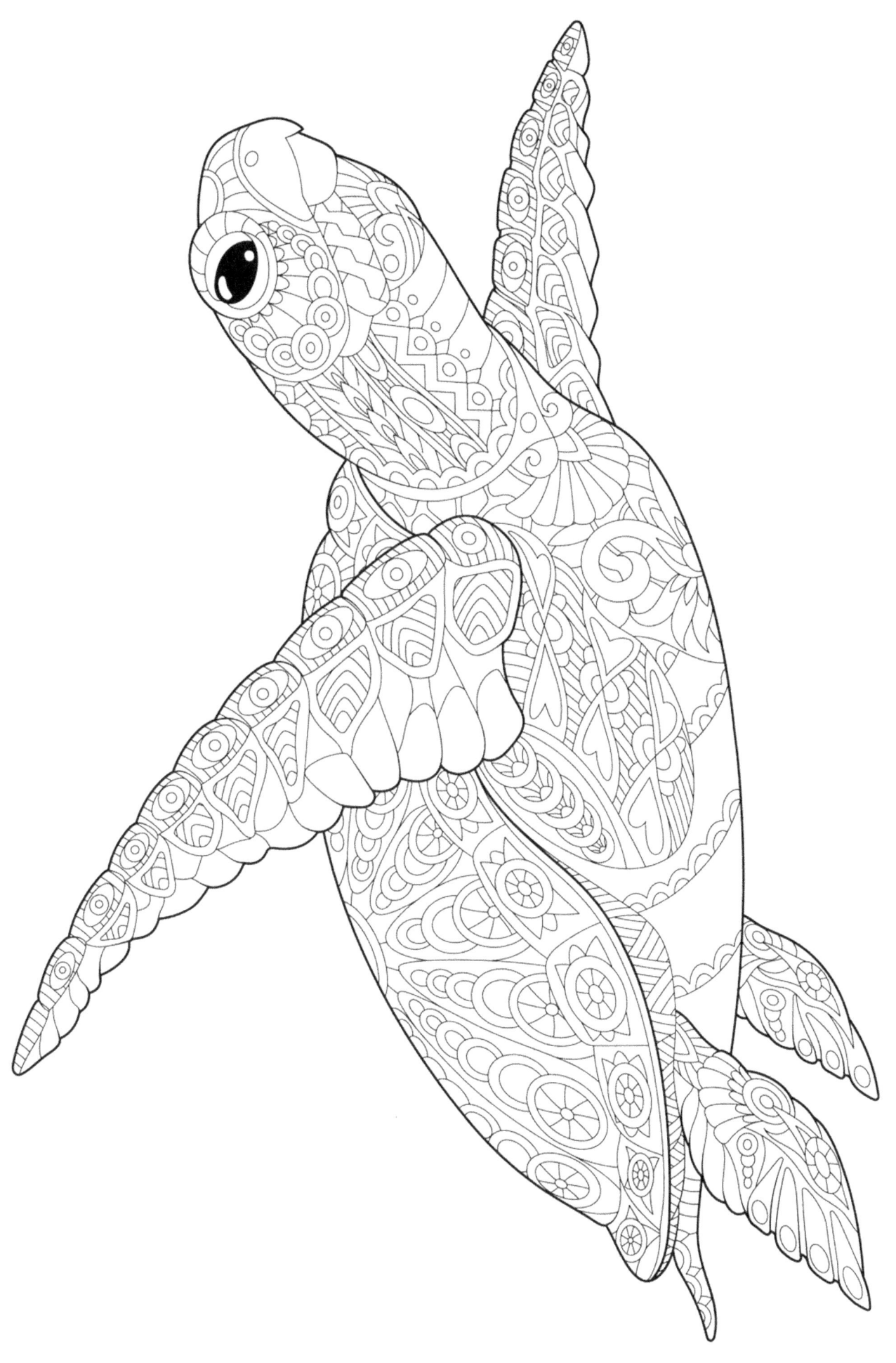

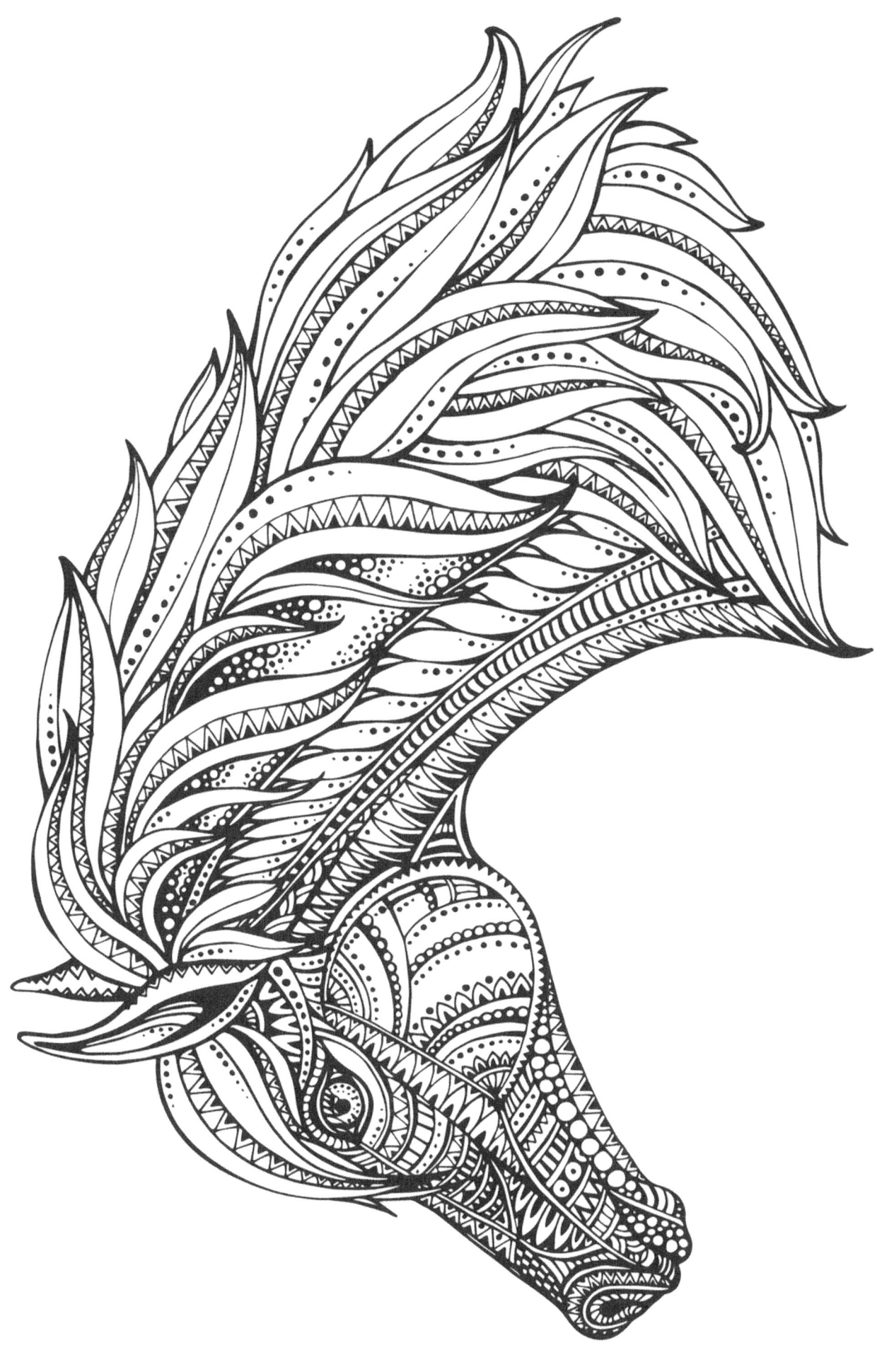

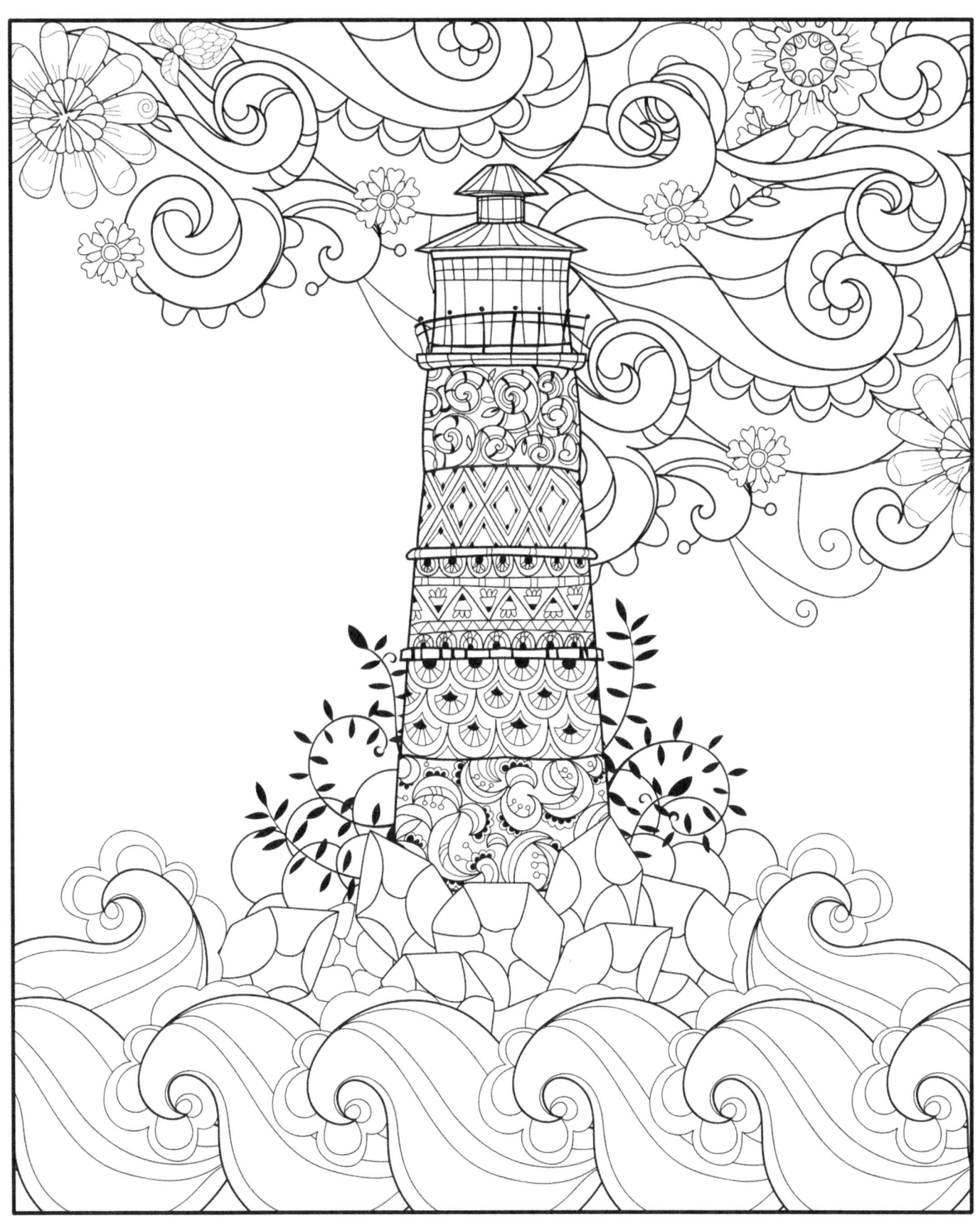

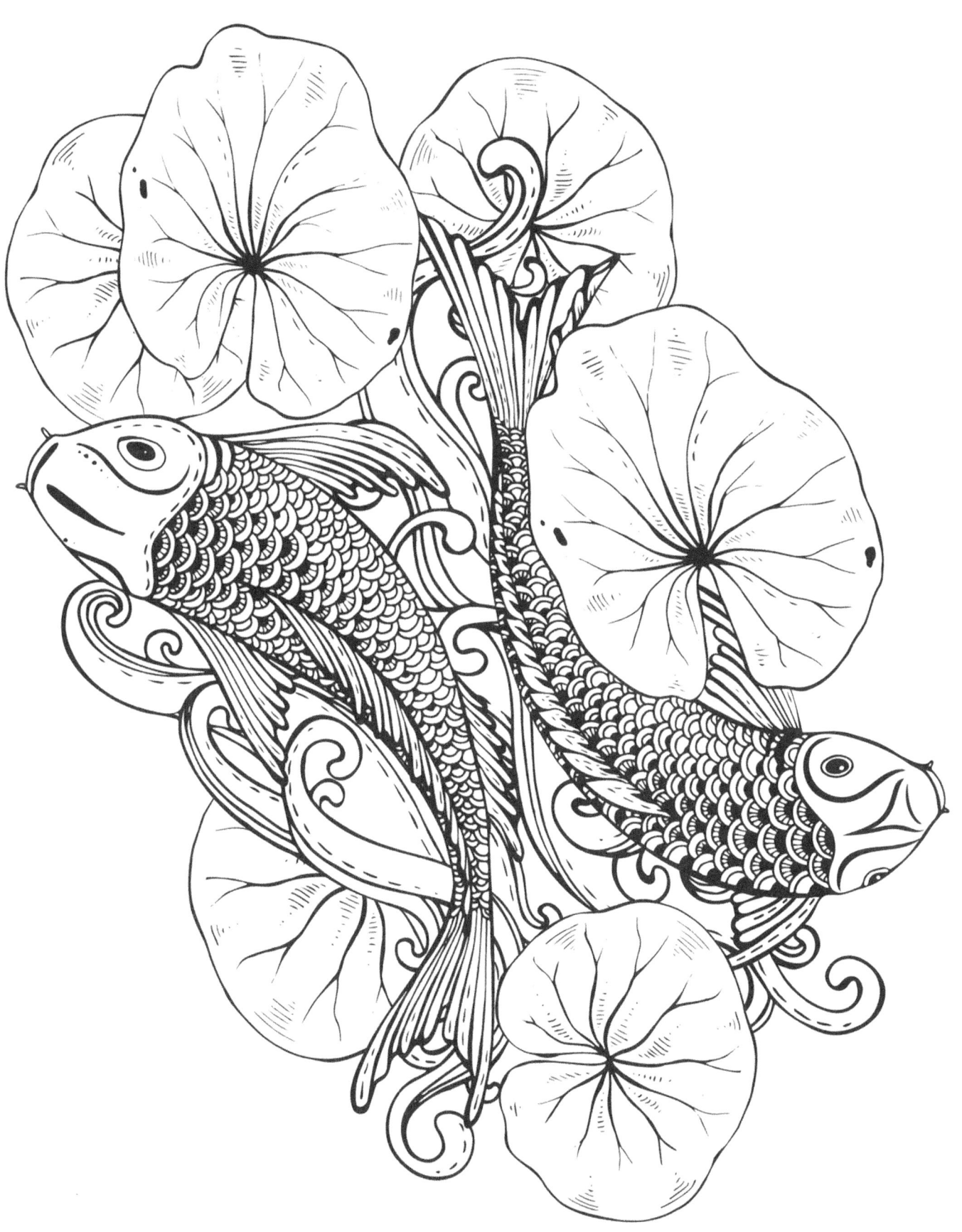

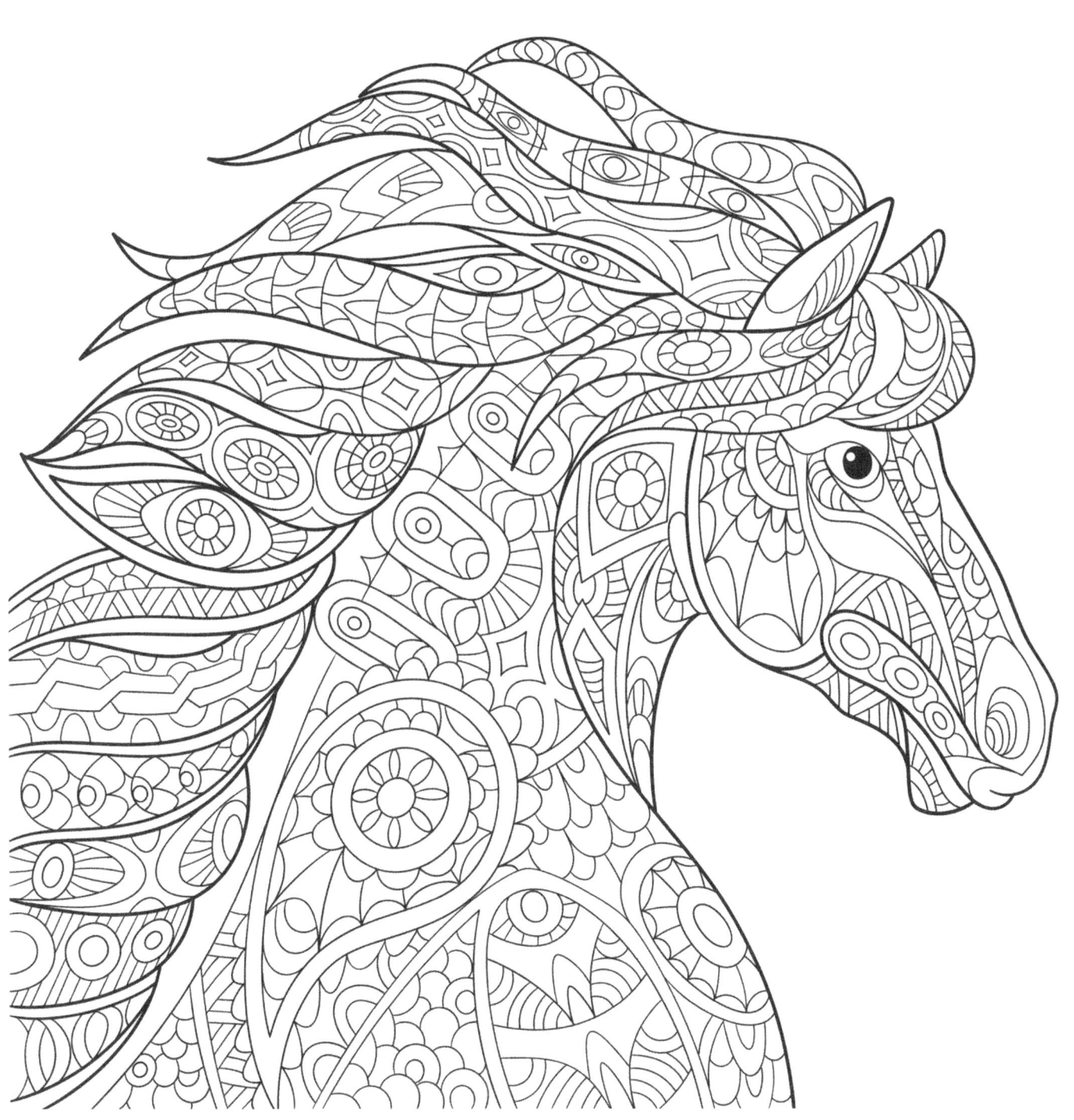

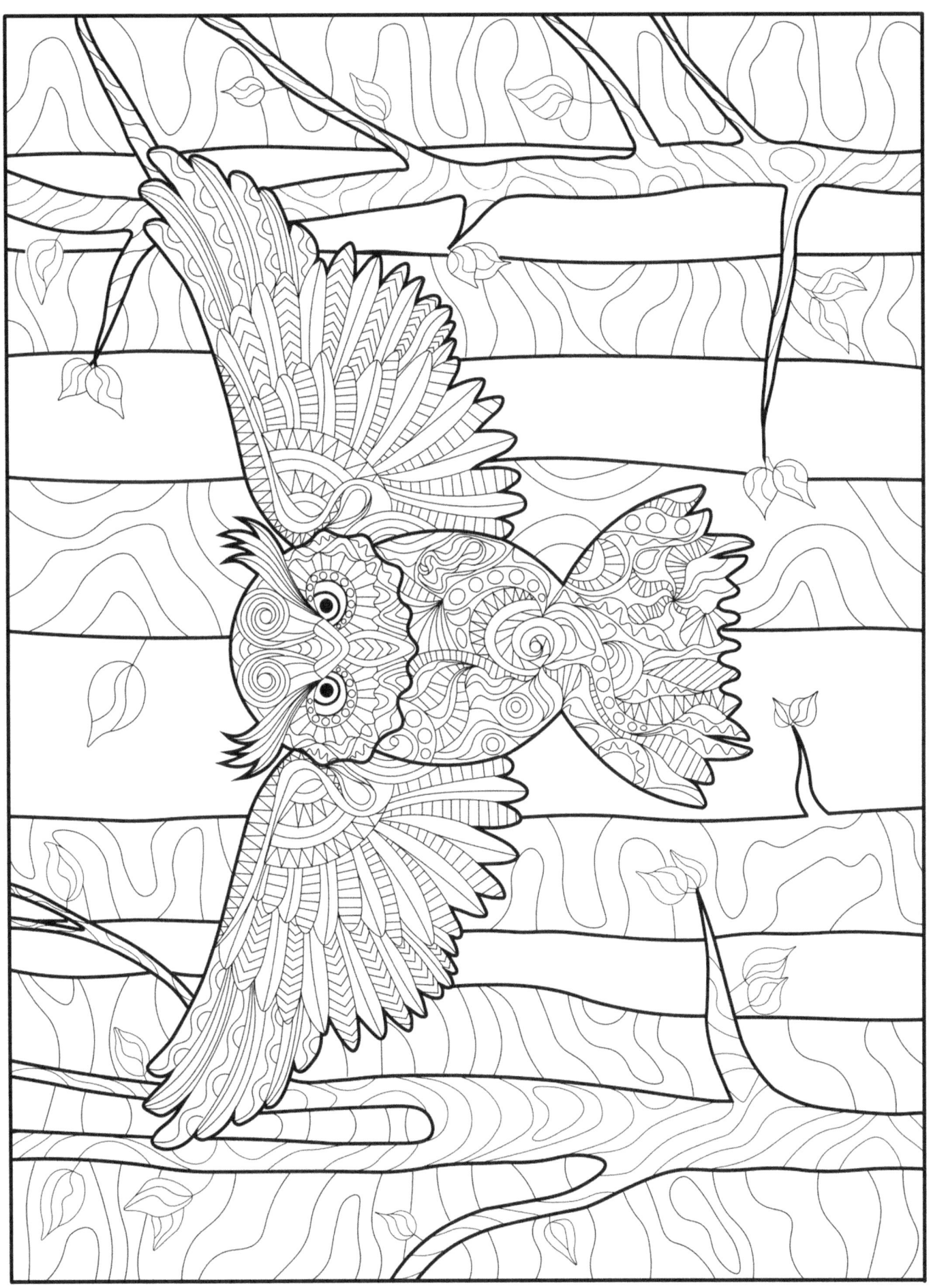

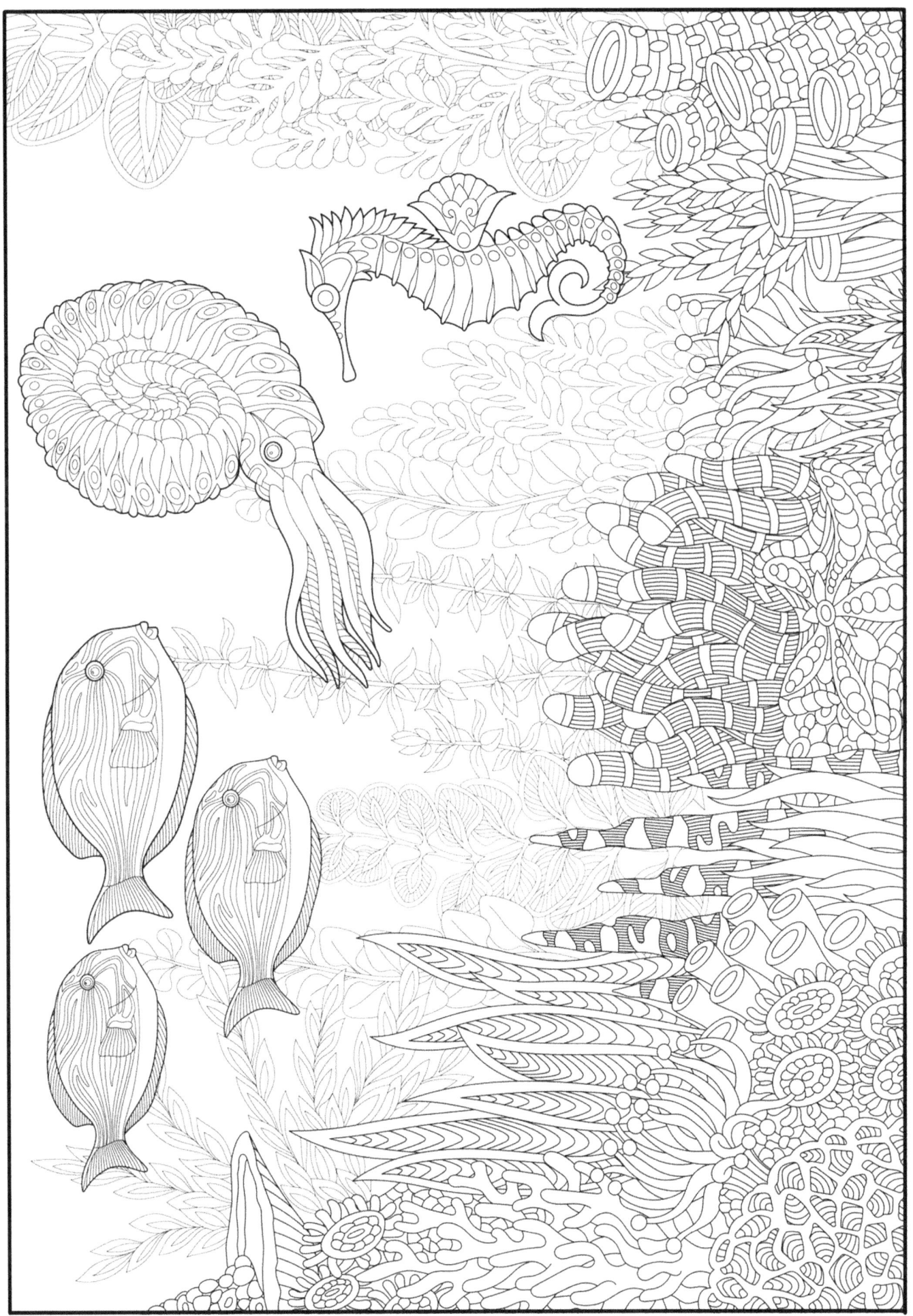

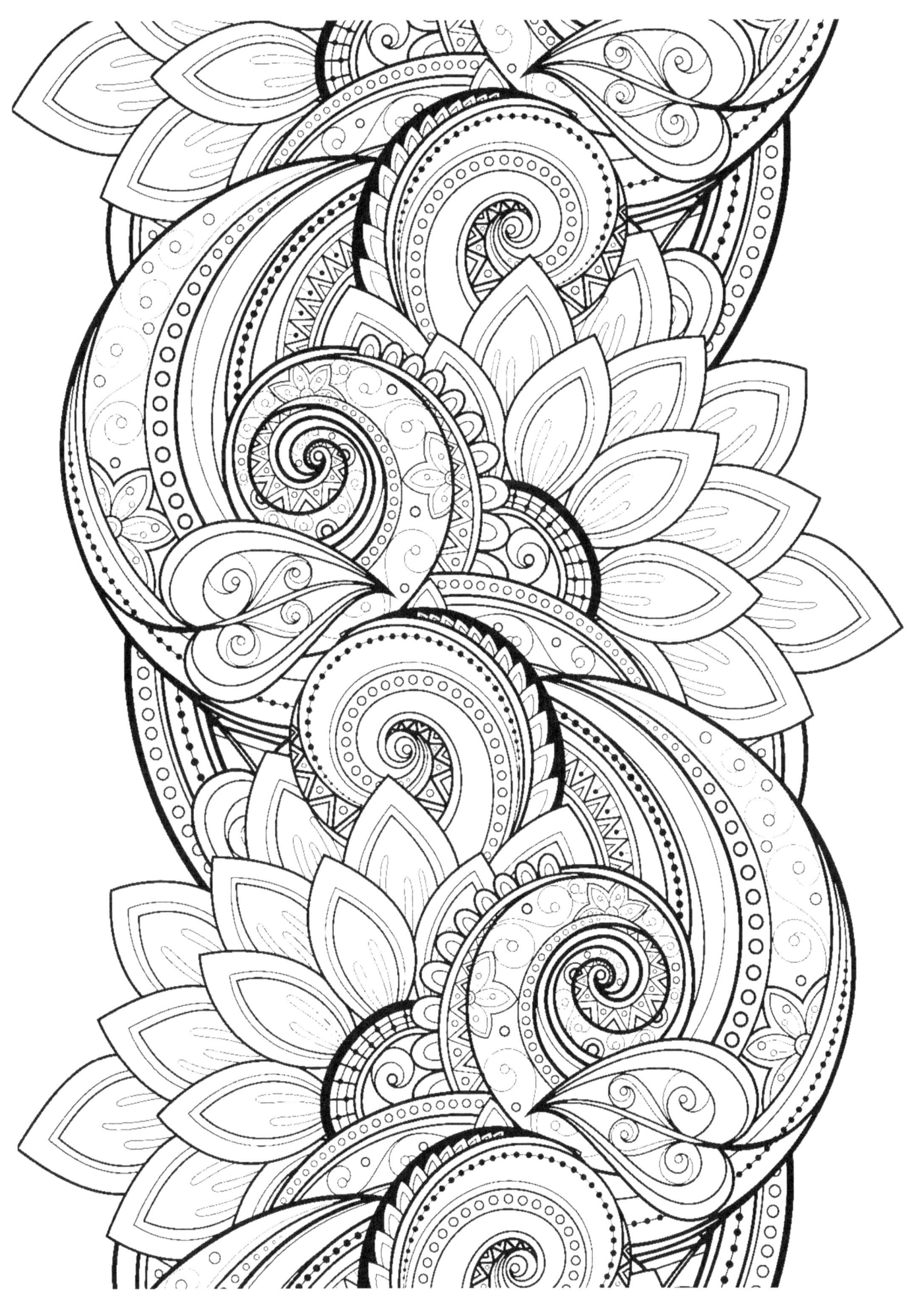

More Coloring Books from Samantha and Friends

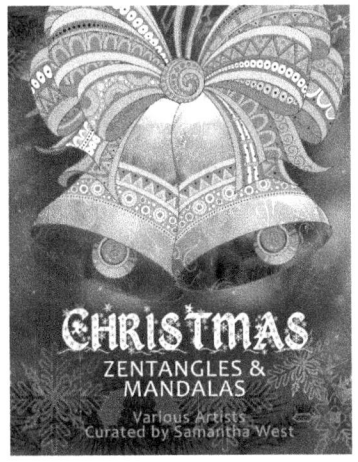

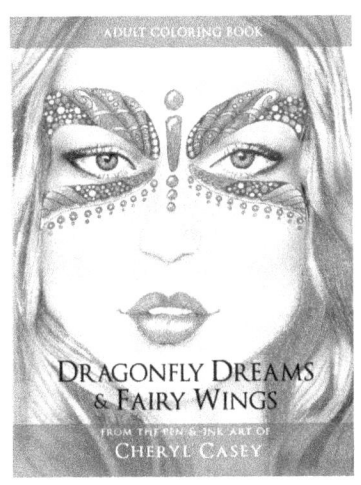

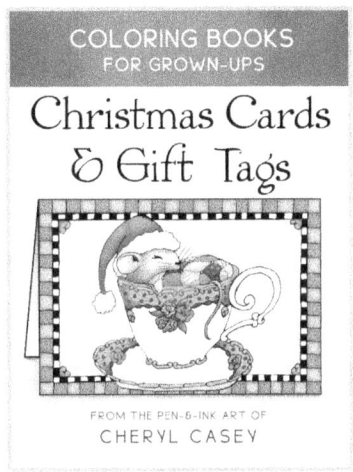

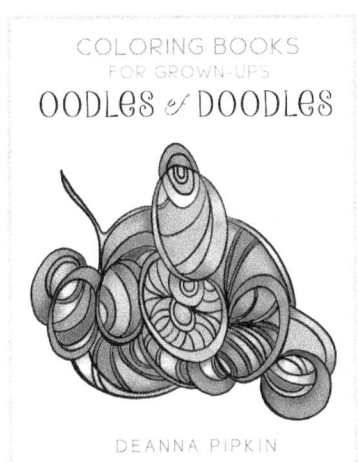

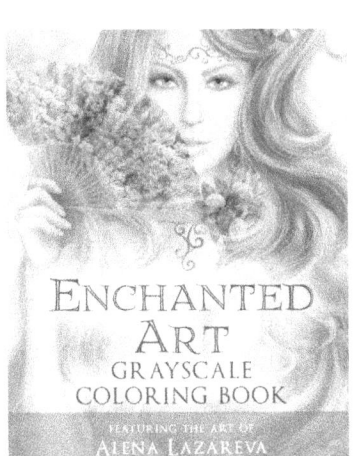

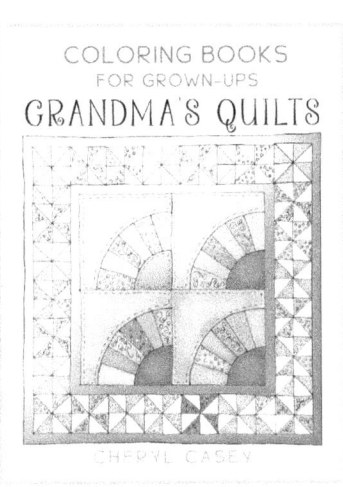

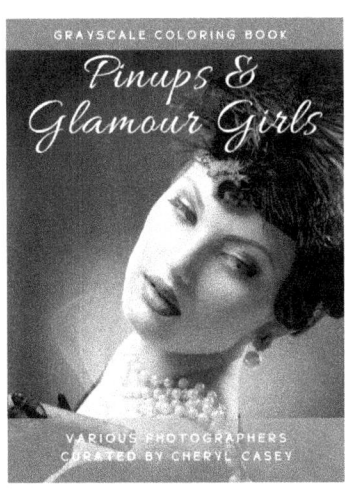

www.ingramcontent.com/pod-product-compliance
Lightning Source LLC
Chambersburg PA
CBHW060010210526
45170CB00017B/2129